Contents

Author's Acknowledgements

I should like to thank the following, particularly, for their help, encouragement, inspiration or advice: Bryn Higgs, Edward Holden, Joseph Hutchinson, Don Johanson, Meave Leakey, Pauline May, John Rodford, Thurstan Shaw, Chris Stringer, William Thorpe, Helga Tomkins and Alan Walker.

Preface

Man has undergone a revolution in the understanding of his origins in the 150 years since the *Beagle* voyage. Darwin not only confirmed the fact of evolution but additionally and importantly unveiled the mechanism whereby organic evolution has unfolded. For the later Victorians the impact of the reality of human descent from the anthropoid apes was cushioned by the inadequacy of the then known human fossils and the imperfectly understood extent of geological time. Throughout this century pieces of the jig-saw puzzle of human descent have been rapidly falling into place, both as the missing links have been found and as the elements in an originally jumbled time scale have been ordered more perfectly by absolute dating techniques. Fossil evidences for at least the past 4.5 million years of human evolution are available in the sediments of the African Great Rift Valley system. From recent hominid discoveries in Africa the physical details of each stage of human descent from ape to man are increasingly clear.

But knowledge of the fossil pattern by no means answers all of the questions about human origins. Neo-Darwinism goes a long way to explain the mechanism of evolutionary change by selection pressure operating on a variable interbreeding population. But the intricacy of this selection process in a social primate with a conscious mind is bound to be more complex in degree if not in kind, for natural selection operates on groups as well as individuals. The human story also manifests a macroevolutionary trend, comparable to the quantum leaps of other kinds in the fossil record. Early hominid changes such as upright walking, the freeing of the hands, social food sharing, extended care of the young, the development of speech, of thought and reflective consciousness all acted together to propel biological and cultural change. The invention of stone tools and the harnessing of material and energy resources, previously untapped by any other animal, enabled man to transform his total environment. Today we can see that the early biological evolutionary changes which lead to man are far distant from the relatively recent events of the Neolithic revolution and the development of the earliest civilisations. Yet our history teaches us that these events were dimly 'long ago'. In this book they constitute the very recent end to a long story.

Thus on the full time scale of the Earth's history, human biological evolution and cultural evolution, in particular, have been explosive in their nature and truly phenomenal in their impact. Students of biology should cultivate an awareness of this fact. The physical and behavioural characteristics of our species, as we find ourselves today, are rooted in the adaptations of our ancestors.

1 Evolution perceived

1.1 Introduction

The picture we have today of man's beginnings and development as a species is one of slow change in form and character over great periods of time. Such a transformation is called **evolution**. The idea of human evolution is still relatively new and we are not yet fully aware of its implications nor has it sufficiently permeated our thinking. Compared with the total evolutionary timescale of millions of years, the origins of agriculture and civilisation, a few thousand years ago, are but recent events. Yet it is a common misjudgement today to consider so-called primitive peoples and the ancients of early history as being, if not dim, certainly not as bright as we are. We adopt this attitude of superiority because we are generally unable to appreciate how they were blind to what we in our time and culture find very obvious. What you have learned since infancy, on your mother's knee, in school, from friends, from books, from television and film has given you a cultural context from which to view the world. A human society's understanding of itself is influenced predominantly by the culture of its own time. We should therefore begin a study of human evolution with a developed awareness of our late twentieth century viewpoint.

All the primitive societies of the modern world, which have been investigated by social anthropologists, have in their tribal folklore a distinct, clearly told, creation story. These stories exist, in part, to answer children's questions as to where the first man and woman came from, which they would be sure to want to know if they had not already been told. The origin of mankind in these creation myths are as varied as they are intriguing. In the Jewish story man is made by God from mud. Anaximander, the early Greek naturalist, was sure that man originally came out of a shark. In India and Ceylon the prevalence of monkey gods suggests another insight. In many of these stories there is an element of divinity either in man himself or in his creator. Also the creation story may establish the cultural context of the people to whom it belongs, hence consequent upon Adam and Eve's creation we learn of their 'fall', an expression of their conscious self-awareness and consequent obligation to follow a moral order. Such perception of human nature could only come from modern minds like ours.

The orthodox views of early Christian civilisation in Europe were based upon the old creation insights of the Jewish story and the classical writings of the later Greeks. Plato's arbitration on early Greek ideas of creation had been that species were immutable (unable to change or evolve); this is not surprising for nobody had seen one species turn into another. In the Renaissance, the concept of a creator God who set things in motion with a purpose, which was the Jewish idea, now combined with such Greek logical thinking. Thus it was argued that if God had made things to work, then the mechanism could be observed. Leonardo da Vinci and Vesalius began investigations of human anatomy and of natural history that introduced a clearer understanding of man's affinity to animals and to the apes. By the nineteenth century, knowledge of the great apes was such that all were agreed that they were anatomically and physically very close to man but spiritually different. The early scientific name for the chimpanzee, *Pan satyrus*, implied a semi-divine yet semi-bestial human; a paradox from which thinking people could not escape.

In Sweden during the mid-eighteenth century **Carl von Linné** (Carolus Linnaeus, in his latinised form) developed an hierarchical classification system for describing the great variety of plants and animals that were daily arriving in Europe as a result of global exploration. In his *Systema Natura* of 1740 Linnaeus grouped organisms according to their degree of physical similarity. Man was grouped with other man-like or anthropoid apes as a **Primate**, the highest ranking order of mammals. Linnaeus was a conservative in that he regarded species as immutable, although he did have some trouble with placing hybrid plants in his system. He was certainly initially unaware that his tree-like construct for classification might be read as a tree of physical ascent in time. The Linnaean system was so much more practical than anything that had preceded it that it was soon in use throughout Europe. In pre-Revolutionary France, a group of distinguished natural scientists, led by the seemingly conservative aristocrat le Compte de Buffon, adopted the Linnaean system as just such a blue-print for evolution. Buffon's pupil, **Jean Baptiste Lamark**, who survived the guillotine, was the first proponent of a theory to account for such a postulated evolution of plants and animals, for in the radical atmosphere of post-Revolutionary France such ideas were possible. Evolutionary ideas spread to England along with radical political thought. These ideas were thus discussed in liberal households in England before the end of the eighteenth century. An English doctor called Erasmus Darwin was sufficiently intrigued by the subject of evolution to write and no doubt suggestively talk of it. His grandson, Charles, was to find a mechanism to explain such change and live to see evolutionary theory accepted in his own lifetime. Darwin was an undoubted genius and yet even the cultural context of his own upbringing did not enable him to see certain truths at all easily.

A particular framework of scientific thought in which one is culturally reared is called a **paradigm**. From what has been said so far, it will be seen that the paradigm one is reared in can enable you to see new relationships or truths and yet cloud your view of what, to someone later, may be obvious. In reading this book you need to become more aware of the 'paradigm problem' for it has often made the story of evolution difficult to tell and hard to follow. Scientific truth has always been an approximation to available evidence. This book aims to set out the consensus view of human evolution, but, as we shall see, if the past is anything to go by some of what is written here will prove to be misleading or incorrect in the future! This cannot be avoided. We can only proceed stepwise with the knowledge we have.

1.2 Evidences for evolution

There are many clear accounts of the evidences for the fact of evolutionary change, quite apart from the evidences of the mechanism of such change. These may be found in standard biology course books and in others referred to in Further Reading at the end of this book. The evidence for the fact of evolution has not always been easy to interpret for those faced with it. Today you have probably been brought up to believe in the fact of evolution, so much so that you may accept it uncritically. This would be a pity. Have you, for example, ever unearthed a fossil from its bedded position? Conversely, you may have been reared in an attitude of hostility to evolutionary theory. You may have learned that fossils have been planted by the devil to divert people from the truth of the biblical Origin and **Special Creation** of 4004 BC. Special Creation can neither be disproved nor proved scientifically for it does not allow any predictions to be tested experimentally. Evolutionary theory is based on observation and deduction and in part upon experiments. Its strength lies in its plausibility.

Geochronology

The antiquity of the Earth is in many ways the most striking feature of its geology. Two centuries ago James Hutton noted that many of the bedded rocks, or **geological strata** as they are called, were clearly the result of erosionary and depository forces still at work today. Charles Lyell followed Hutton with his observation that lower strata, by virtue of their position, must be older than those above them. Owing to the fortuitous tilted bedding of the British Isles such early British geologists were able to compute that the Earth's crust must, for the time taken for it to form, be at least four million years old. At its first conception, this seemed a long time. It was after all one thousand times longer than the prediction made from a rigorous counting of generation times in the Old Testament. Current estimates of the age of the Earth are intriguingly one thousand times greater than Lyell's and centre on a date of about four and a half thousand million years before the present (4 500 Ma). Such recent estimates are derived from the decremental decay rates of radioactive isotopes (see Chapter 5).

Throughout this book time is expressed in years before present (a), unless otherwise stated (1 Ma = 10^6 years).

Palaeontology

Within many geological strata are bedded the actual remains, transformed mineralised remains, or just traces, of once-living things. Such fossils show several striking things that accord with evolutionary ideas. Firstly, the oldest rocks have creatures different from and more primitive than those alive today, whilst higher and more recent strata frequently contain forms that are modern or almost so. Most exciting to a palaeontologist is that from lower strata to higher ones it is occasionally possible to follow changes in one continuous evolutionary line. The most famous example of such **phyletic evolution** is that of the horses, *Equidae*, of North America during the Tertiary age of the Cenozoic era. A small, three-toed terrier-sized creature, *Hyracotherium*, is, by a series of successively larger forms, found to be ancestral to a pony-sized modern horse, *Equus*, with considerable changes in the tooth shape and a reduction in

4

the number of digits on each foot. This transformation of a small three-toed browser to a large single-toed grazer is dramatic in form but must have been imperceptibly slow for most of the time if one recognises the Tertiary duration of 60 Ma. The fossil record is of course only clearly shown by painstaking excavation and happy (for us) accidents of preservation. Although the record is like a film lasting for hours from which a few still frames survive, careful analyses of these can tell you much about the events that took place in the full extent of geological time. Intriguingly some fossils provide a bridging function between two different forms alive today. Such fossils are rather dramatically called 'missing links', a term badly over used in popular descriptions of fossil man.

Geographical distribution

The geographical distribution of existing plants and animals is a third pillar of evolutionary evidence. Travellers in the last century became increasingly aware that each of the major continents had different assemblages of animals and plants. Although they may have had similar habitats, of swamps, plains, forests, foothills and mountains with comparable climates and environmental conditions, the animals and plants which they held were different. Within one continental environment all the niches of the habitats were filled by species for which there was a counterpart in the same environment in a different continent. Alfred Wallace, a contributor to Darwin's theory of evolution, noted that the geographically closer the isolated faunas were, the greater the number of common forms they possessed. From these observations it seemed increasingly clear that migrations of plants and animals were free until a continent became isolated by the sea or some other barrier of ice or mountain range and that over a long period of time forms had evolved to fit all of the ecological niches available. This **adaptive radiation** of life can best be explained by evolution, as is so clearly expressed by Darwin in the thoughts that came to him on the Galapagos Islands in 1834 when considering the finches he had studied. 'Seeing this gradation and diversity of structure in one small, intimately related group of birds, one might really fancy that from an original shortage of birds in this archipelago, one species has been taken and modified for different ends.'

Embryology

An examination of the embryological stages of development in animals, at the end of the last century, led the German biologist Ernst Haekel to support evolutionary views. He claimed that the development of zygotes to adult forms repeated the pathway of evolutionary development from protozoan to modern forms of vertebrate. Individual development, in other words, repeats the phylogenetic developments of evolution. Today we view this **Theory of Recapitulation** as being over-stretched and simplistic, but there are undoubted similarities between the early stages of vertebrate embryos which we cannot ignore. Without some recognition of this theory one is hard put to explain why the human embryo, a few weeks old, has such a well-developed tail and clefts in the pharynx wall in a manner closely similar to the equivalent embryonic

10 000	9000	8000	7000	6000	5000	4000
Origin of the solar system					Earliest rock formations on earth	Origin of life on earth
					◁————————ARCHEAN EON————	

stage of a fish. At a later stage of human development a complete covering of fine hair is formed on the foetus, only then to be shed before birth!

Comparative anatomy

Again, if one only takes evolution as an hypothesis one can argue that organisms related in a tree-like manner should have common structures to which one can point. In reviewing a taxonomic group such as the mammals, such comparative anatomy can highlight a common basic structure such as the five-fingered (or toed) limb. This pentadactyl limb is a **homologous** structure, common to all mammals, but is modified for different uses in the hand of man, the wing of a bat, the flipper of a whale or the front foot of an elephant. In each case the digits may be found and numbered and shown to have the same constituent bones, the phalanges, metacarpals and carpals. Such homologies have of course been used to produce the Linnaean system, so it is a derived argument to use the classifactory system *per se* as a support for evolution, but none the less a valid one for kinship given the implications of homologous structures. Homologies, in an accepted evolutionary context, also help to explain anatomical anomalies such as the seemingly useless intestinal appendix of man, which in various herbivorous primates is a functional digestive chamber. Other vestigial organs such as the pelvic girdle and femur bones of the python are convincing evidence of evolutionary change.

Comparative physiology and biochemistry

Recent knowledge of physiology and biochemistry supports evolution as well. If anatomical features show homology, so too do the biomolecules constructed in living organisms through the mediation of their genetic system. Such molecules as ATP and DNA are universal to all cellular organisms, whilst the phosphocreatine of muscle is common to all chordates, but not to the majority of invertebrates. Analysis of the amino acid sequencing in biomolecules, such as cytochrome, indicates close affinity of genetic relatedness for organisms seen to be similar on other criteria in the Linnaean classification. Such biochemical studies or immunological studies on the relatedness of blood sera is as compelling as the evidence of anatomical homology. So close is the chimpanzee to man, by these criteria, as to cause some biochemists with their faith in **molecular clocks** to question whether the chimpanzee is not a closer relative of man than the fossil evidence suggests.

1.3 The origin of life

If one is to accept the fact of evolution, two intellectual questions must then be put and satisfactory answers found to them. How was it possible for life to start and by what evolutionary mechanism does it change? Darwin provided for us

3000	2500	2000	1750	1500	1250	1000
Photosynthesis begins	Algal fossils			Origin of eukaryotic cells		

PROTEROZOIC EON

much of the answer to the second question and this will be looked at critically in the following chapters. The actual origin of life, however, is a puzzle but not an insuperable one and certainly not as difficult to conceive of as it was for Darwin over one hundred years ago.

The Earth was physically formed soon after the beginning of our solar system about ten thousand million years ago. By the time that half of that span had elapsed life had most probably begun. Judging from our present knowledge of the solar system's planets the Earth is unusual. Had it been nearer or further from the Sun it would probably not have had its clothing of seas and water vapour. The physical properties of water are such as to reduce the great fluctuations of surface temperatures that we know to occur on planets without seas and water-laden atmospheres. Our moist atmosphere also filters out unduly damaging radiations. Such an ecological homeostasis for thousands of millions of years has made the evolution of life more plausible here than elsewhere in our solar system at least. On the basis of spectral analysis of the atmospheres of planets such as Jupiter, astronomers have postulated a chemically reducing atmosphere for the primitive Earth. Ammonia, methane, hydrogen and water, heated by volcanism and radiation and sparked through by lightning discharge could in theory produce seas of dissolved amino acids and other simple organic molecules. Stanley Miller, in a now classical experiment in 1953, replicated this atmosphere and these conditions and thereby synthesised amino acids in his Chicago laboratory.

If one looks at the molecules common to all living things, the nucleic acids and proteins and their respective constituent units, the nucleotides and amino acids, we may find the possible key. An energised nucleotide, with two added phosphate groups, is ATP, the pivotal molecule in all energy transformations in cells. Yet the same nucleotides, as the nucleic acid polymers, provide not only a system of replication of prebiotic life, but also carry a coding system for the assembly of amino acids into proteins. In the role of enzymes, proteins may further catalyse syntheses and the release of energy from chemical bonds. A **primordial soup** of nucleotides and amino acids, with a source of energy such as light or that in other pre-formed organic molecules, could conceivably, by the operation of a pre-biotic natural selection, give rise to simple life forms. Such submicroscopic entities would have needed to have had a capacity for growth and accurate replication, and a means of harnessing and transforming energy in their environment to their own ends. They would then have been 'alive'. There were thousands of millions of years for the accident of life but once begun it followed its pattern of accumulating improbabilities. The first definite fossils of simple algal plants from rocks dated 2.5 thousand million years ago suggest that by then cellular forms existed. The slow march of evolution was already well under way.

2 A mechanism for change

2.1 Darwin and natural selection

Charles Darwin (1809–1882) was not the architect of the idea of evolution, nor was he the first person to conceive of a mechanism for such slow change, but he was uniquely placed as a collector of evidence and sifter of ideas and is rightly credited with being the first to lay down the firm basis of our contemporary evolutionary theory. A knowledge of Darwin's thought is essential for an understanding of human origins as well as for any appreciation of the impact of his ideas on recent human history. Within a few years of the publication of the *Origin of species* in 1859 those who followed the author's theory and its implicit beliefs about mankind's origins called themselves 'Darwinians'. Today we use the term **Darwinism** to describe this original exposition. However, our understanding of the processes of biological change has been so deepened and freshened by further confirming evidence that the modern synthesis is often called **Neo-Darwinism**, to distinguish it.

Darwin's early life is well documented in several excellent biographies which students of biology should read. The influences which combined together in Darwin's mind to enable him to conceive of an evolutionary mechanism were several. He had an excellent boyhood training as a naturalist and, showing no aptitude for medicine or theology whilst a student, he became a gentleman-naturalist collector on the five year voyage of the *Beagle* around the world. Darwin's Beagle journal shows clearly that by the age of 24 he had appreciated that species had been transformed both in time, through the fossil record, and divergently on the different islands which he visited. Returning home in 1836 he had an immense store of memories and records to draw upon. A second influence of importance was that of his paternal grandfather, Erasmus, whose evolutionary works Charles certainly studied on returning from his voyage, if not before. The family memory of Erasmus must have been strong, with his meal-time aphorism to the children that the First Law of Nature was 'Eat or be Eaten'. But Charles Darwin reading *An essay on populations* by **Robert Malthus**, written in the same revolutionary period as his grandfather's work, was struck by the germ of a new idea. Malthus' observations were socio-economic not biological. He had argued that if the standard of living of the poor was raised, they would inevitably increase in number. As population was known to increase faster than the means of production, at that time, living standards would inevitably fall back to the old level. Man was therefore doomed in poverty to 'a struggle for existence'. Two years after his world voyage Darwin relates his breakthrough:

> I happened to read for my amusement *Malthus on population* and being well prepared to appreciate the struggle for existence, which from my long continued observations of the habits of animals and plants everywhere goes

on, it at once struck me that under the circumstances favourable variations would tend to be preserved and unfavourable ones to be destroyed. The result of this would be the formation of new species.

Variations and heritability he had observed in nature, now with Malthus' 'struggle' in his mind Darwin conceived the solution to his puzzle.

Over the following years Darwin built up his theory, but he was remorselessly plagued by self-doubt and indecision. He early confided his ideas to a close group of friends and gained strong support from Lyell, a geologist, and Hooker, a botanist, both of them outstanding scientists in their fields. On the one hand Darwin was convinced that his theory was correct, but on the other he could not bring himself to face the consequences of such a theory being publicly debated, for implicit in the theory must be a common ancestry for apes and men. After 20 years, in 1858, Darwin's hand at last was forced. Alfred Wallace, fellow naturalist and later famed zoogeographer, wrote to Darwin spelling out a theory which was an almost identical exposition of his own ideas. Lyell had warned Darwin that he would lose his place as architect of the theory if he did not now act. Wallace and Darwin thus published a brief joint paper, to be followed a year later by Darwin's *Origin of Species*. As he had expected, Darwin was indeed reviled and caricatured by the press but by the time of his death in 1882 he had earned a place for himself amongst the great Victorians, and was buried in Westminster Abbey.

Darwin's theory of **evolution by natural selection** is most simply set down as propositions based upon observations and as the deductions from them.

Observation A: All known species produce more offspring than are required to replace them; they overproduce.

Observation B: The population of a species, apart from fluctuations about a mean, tends to have a fairly constant level; populations are stable.

Deduction 1: There is therefore a struggle for existence; many individuals perish before reproducing themselves.

Observation C: Organisms produce offspring which resemble their parents closely; like produces like.

Observation D: Organisms are variable and the offspring of any two parents reproducing sexually will be varied; like may produce unlike.

Deduction 2: In any species there is variation which is inheritable; this is the nature of heredity.

Each of the paired observations appear at first to contradict, but each pair finds a synthesis in the deductions which follow.

Darwin's achievement was to draw these two deductions further together to build a theory of 'the survival of the fittest'. He argued that since there is a **struggle for existence** among individuals, and since these individuals are not all alike, some of the variations among them will be advantageous in the struggle for survival, others unfavourable. Consequently a higher proportion of individuals with favourable variations will on the average survive to

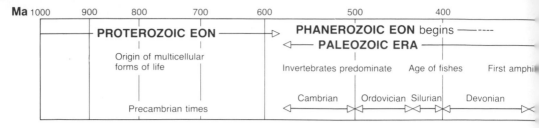

reproduce; a higher proportion of those with unfavourable variations will die before reproducing. Since variation is transmitted by heredity, the effects of differential survival will accumulate with each generation. This **natural selection** (constrasted to the **artificial selection** used by man on domestic species) will act constantly to improve the adaptation of a species to its environment and may in the course of time generate a new species entirely.

Darwin's theory held against the inevitable criticism of his fellow scientists. The weakest part of his argument was over the nature of heredity, for this had neither the light of Mendelism upon it nor any straightforward theory of mutation to account for the origins of the new variations he had observed to occur. Darwin was not even sure whether the simplest organism did not have a blueprint within it, unexpressed, for some later pattern of evolution. Whatever his conceptual difficulty he was not imperceptive. He understood chance to play a great part in heredity. He made it clear that the occurrence of variation must have a cause. In the absence of a clear hypothesis he therefore came to mix his views with Lamark's much earlier ideas of the inheritance of acquired characteristics, which he was eventually inclined to feel might be involved. Lamark had attributed evolutionary change to adaptive modifications during the life of the individual which affected the inheritance in such a way that offspring grew up already somewhat modified in this adaptive direction. **Lamarkism** has repeatedly been entertained as a possible additive influence to natural selection. However, it has never really stood up to rigorous investigation although its influence in evolutionary biology is felt to this day. Before the later editions of *Origin of species* appeared, a German biologist, Weismann, made some important steps in clearing Darwinism of this Lamarkian confusion. Amongst the experiments he carried out was one in which the tails of mice were removed from the animals, at birth, for many successive generations. Not surprisingly, you may think, the mice continued to be born with undiminished tail lengths. Weissman attributed this to inheritance through the reproductive cells alone, cells set aside in the embryo of an individual and thus not much influenced by the course of that individual's life. This theory of the continuity of the germ plasm, in essence, still holds today.

2.2   Darwinism and Neo-Darwinism

Darwin might have tumbled to genetical theory had he adopted **Gregor Mendel's** strategy of following the inheritance of one or a few inheritable traits through a number of generations. Darwin certainly conceived that there might be particles, or gemmules, to be passed from one generation to the next but he saw them as equally blending in the contributions from the two parents. Mendel's work, although contemporary with Darwin's, was not known

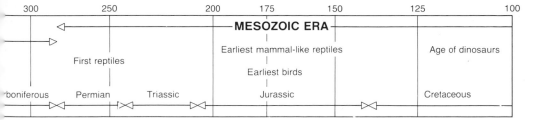

300	250	200	175	150	125	100

MESOZOIC ERA

Earliest mammal-like reptiles

First reptiles

Earliest birds

Age of dinosaurs

| boniferous | Permian | Triassic | Jurassic | Cretaceous |

outside his native Austria. Mendel discovered the genetic dominance and recessiveness of characters and by revealing mathematically their paired nature he anticipated the discovery of allelic genes on homologous chromosomes. Before the end of the nineteenth century the importance of mutation in evolutionary change was beginning to be recognised. The work of de Vries in this respect was important. Indeed so ardent were the **mutation theory** proponents that natural selection declined in significance as an evolutionary explanation. When Mendel's work of 1866 was rediscovered, in 1900, the science of genetics was born with explosive force. Not only were the rules of inheritance found to be applicable to all sexually reproducing plants and animals but the actual particulate gene ceased to be elusive and become a localised, identifiable reality. By 1916 Bridges and Morgan had formulated a **chromosome theory of inheritance** that was able to pinpoint actual genes to specific loci on the homologous chromosomes of the fruit fly *Drosophila*. Mutant genes could be shown to exist in these positions, and by inference, such normal variations might occur in nature and be subject to the natural selection Darwin had anticipated. So swift was the appreciation of these ideas of genes as independent elements moving within the wider gene pool of an interbreeding species that it is hard to appreciate the suddenness of this second revolution in thinking. In 1908 G. H. Hardy and W. Weinberg independently developed a relatively simple mathematical concept to describe the equilibrium of genes in a population of organisms. This **Hardy-Weinberg theorem** is discussed in the next chapter, for it gives some important insights into our understanding of human evolution and of modern evolutionary theory.

Darwinism is a term used to express the observational and deductive method which gave rise to the theory of evolution. Darwinism has been freed from any confusion with Lamarkism and been added to by the insights of twentieth century genetics. Thus our present understanding of breeding systems, of Darwinian fitness and of the effects of selection upon the genetic composition of species have all contributed to the theory. In this new form it has been called **Neo-Darwinism**, and is a pillar of modern biology. Like any ruling orthodoxy we should endeavour to see that its predominance does not cloud what must be the essentially verifiable nature of experimental science. Neo-Darwinism has become so established that rightly some have questioned its predominance in our thinking. Is it a paradigm, or scientific framework of ideas, which might prevent us from seeing new truths about human origins? The present controversy over **cladism** is a case in point. Most biologists welcome such novel ideas but are confident that Neo-Darwinism has still much to offer our understanding of human origins.

The appreciation of Darwinism was a major event in man's discovery of himself. In 1860 Adam Sedgwick, the eminent Victorian geologist, in reviewing the *Origin of species* ventured the prophecy that if Darwin's ideas were accepted humanity 'would suffer a damage that might brutalize it and sink the human race into a lower state of degradation than any to which it has fallen since written records tell us of its history'. For these sentiments Darwin thought him a prejudiced 'old bird' but it is sadly true that Darwinism has since been used to colour some interpretations of society and of political relationships. A **Social Darwinism**, with survival of the fittest as its cry has been used to justify ruthless economic competition and racialist policies. These are political conveniences, however, and are not something that we can honestly hold against Darwin himself. On the positive side it can be said that our current appreciation of evolution has given us a much longer perspective on human history. We can thus learn a great deal about our nature by looking back. Darwin also has provided us with a mechanism to explain how such change is possible; how we came to be. But the truth is out. Biologically we are animals, yet in some indefinable way we are set aside in degree, if not in kind, from all other organisms.

Figure 2.1

3 The genetic basis of human evolution

There would not have been so much difficulty over the understanding of evolution if it had been possible to sit down and watch it happening. The problem was, and is, that it is all just too slow. If, however, Darwin's theory is carefully examined, in conjunction with a knowledge of modern genetics, there is much that can be seen to demonstrate the processes of slow evolutionary change.

3.1 The origin of variations

First, the **origin of variations** and the way in which variability is increased must be appreciated. Man has 23 pairs of chromosomes and similar numbers are found in all the higher primates to which we may be related by several million years of descent from a common ape-like ancestor. It is clear that within this assemblage of genetic information some **chromosomal mutations** will have occurred to produce change. There is good evidence that chromosomal deletions, translocations and duplications have occurred and still do occur in the human genome. Translocations, though often harmful, are quite common and duplication of genes must have occurred in the past to account for such things as the three adjacent loci for three different haemoglobin proteins on one chromosome. Chromosomes, however, are only vehicles for genes and it is **mutant genes** that provide the most frequently occurring novel variations in evolution.

For obvious reasons the understanding of our own species' genetics is more hazy than that for *Drosophila*, but Penrose, on the basis of studies in man on the occurrence of dominant mutations such as achondroplasia which are immediately phenotypically shown, estimates that the mutation rate for each gene locus is between 10^{-5} and 10^{-6} per gamete produced. Assuming only 50 000 loci to a chromosome, with our 23 pairs it is apparent that each gamete may have at least one newly mutant gene and possibly more. It would seem that new mutations, albeit mostly recessive and harmful, are therefore quite common. Each of us probably has a new mutant gene for something! The antiquity of many of our genetic systems is again indicated by the occurrence of some identical blood proteins and the presence of the ABO blood group system in the great apes.

3.2 The spread of genes

If a new mutant gene has arisen by chance and is potentially of advantage to an individual, such a tiny biochemical change in DNA coding, a miniscule event, cannot possibly affect the course of evolution in that individual's species unless a number of major sequential events occur. First, the gene must find **expression**; it must operate within the genotype to affect the phenotype.

Secondly, the altered phenotype must have a higher **fitness**, in a Darwinian sense, than other phenotypes, that is the individual must survive and breed to pass on its gene. Thirdly, successful breeding is essential for the gene to be replicated into a larger population of individuals. How this occurs in the **mating system** of the species may have some effect upon the expression of the gene and hence the fitness it confers. It is important to get to grips with these micro-evolutionary events for they form the whole functional basis of the major evolutionary process.

Darwinian fitness is not just a question of survival but one of the individual contributing more offspring to the next generation than other individuals. This fitness may involve just a single member of the species or the whole social group to which that individual belongs. The fitness of the individual is the easiest concept to grasp. Survival from zygote to reproductive age is generally the greatest difficulty to be faced, but if survivorship here is high success in reproduction and fertility may be more significant. The general idea of fitness is illustrated for man, in Britain today, by Penrose (1976) who estimates that of all conceptions 15% die early in pregnancy, 3% are still-born, neonatal deaths account for a further 2%, whilst 3% more fail to reach maturity. Of those who grow to maturity 20% do not marry at all and of those that do 10% remain childless. From this example alone it can be seen how complex the process of selection can be and how many different kinds of genetic feature may be involved.

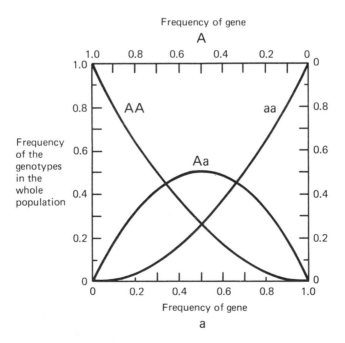

Figure 3.1 The relationship between the frequency of a pair of allelic genes and the frequency of their three possible combinant genotypes in a population.
(The graph is read by considering a vertical line at a particular gene frequency. The frequency of the genotype, at this gene frequency, may then be read off from the vertical scale.)

3.3   Genes in a population

Before the fitness of a single gene can be considered it will be necessary to review the manner in which genes occur in individuals, as genes and genotypes, and in the genetic pool of a species. The vast majority of genes have a partner gene or allele on the corresponding homologous chromosome to that on which they themselves are found. These segregate independently in gamete formation but recombine in pairs in each individual to make the genotypes which altogether form the genome or total genetic complement. The frequency of occurrence of a gene in the **gene pool** of a randomly interbreeding population and the frequency of occurrence of the genotype combinations are related together by the **Hardy-Weinberg equations**, or graphically by Figure 3.1. This figure considers two alleles **A** and **a** and their combinant genotypes **AA**, **Aa** and **aa**. The equilibrium between gene and genotype frequency, predicted by the Hardy-Weinberg theorem, for any population possessing these two alleles will correspond to a vertical line drawn down the figure. At such a point the gene frequencies of **a** and **A** will sum to 1.0 and the relative frequencies of the genotypes in the population, shown at the intersection of the selected vertical line and the three curves, will also sum to 1.0. Hardy and Weinberg expressed this reality algebraically instead of graphically by saying: if the frequency of allele $A = p$, and the frequency of allele $a = q$, then $p + q = 1$. If alleles pair at random in the genotypes by the same frequencies which they have as genes, $(p+q) \times (p+q)$ will be the genotype frequencies. As $(p+q)^2 = p^2 + 2pq + q^2$, it will be seen that p^2, $2pq$ and q^2 represent the genotype frequencies of **AA**, **Aa** and **aa** respectively. (Those unfamiliar with these concepts should consult a genetics text book.) Returning to Figure 3.1, it will be apparent that when a genotype frequency is increased or decreased by natural selection, the vertical line, representing the equilibrium, must shift sideways. If particular genotypes are favoured in life their genes, in combination from the pool, will increase in frequency also. When the gene frequency changes then the genotype recombinant frequency in the next generation will shift to reflect the change. Such sideways shifts in equilibrium position may thus only occur in disequilibrial steps. It is these steps which are taken when a new mutant allele is first selected and slowly becomes adopted as the most abundant allele for that locus.

3.4   The selection of fitness

The story of the **peppered moth**, *Biston betularia*, and its change from a pale form to the black melanic form during the industrial revolution is well known. It will serve us here as a particularly good example of gene frequency change. The species occurs in two forms in the English midlands, a variety called *carbonaria* which is black and a variety *typica* which is the peppered grey form from which the species originally gained its name. The melanic *carbonaria* first appeared in 1850 in the soot-polluted environment of Manchester; originally noted by entomologists as rare, it slowly increased in frequency until by 1900 the *typica* form was reduced locally to less than 5% of the population. This striking example of small scale evolution, attributable to an alteration in the organism's environment, has been well nicknamed 'Darwin's missing evidence'. In the 1950s Kettlewell designed experiments to test the hypothesis that the increase in *carbonaria* and decline in *typica* was due to selection, in favour of the black form, by the differential predation of small insectivorous birds visually picking out resting moths on the tree trunks. In a woodland locality near Birmingham, where the trees were somewhat blackened by soot and devoid of their lichen cover, on account of sulphur pollution, he released 802 carefully marked moths of the two varieties. Using a UV light trap he recaptured 239 of these some days later. Table 3.1 shows the results of this investigation.

Whether the *carbonaria* allele (here designated as **A**) was originally dominant we do not know, but it is today. In terms of survival chances in this experiment, *typica* is clearly at a 50% disadvantage, *carbonaria* having twice its fitness. From this information, supposing it to have been a complete generation fitness difference, we may calculate the changed gene frequency from the changed genotype frequency, using the Hardy-Weinberg equations. From Table 3.2 it will be clear that the 50% disadvantage of the homozygous recessive genotype will reduce the frequency of the **a** gene relative to the **A** allele. (The mathematical computation of selection effects need not concern us here, but Kettlewell in this experiment released moths in a ratio corresponding to an equal frequency for each allele, i.e. $p=0.5$, $q=0.5$. With a relative loss of $0.5q^2$, the gene frequency shift is by $\frac{1}{8}$th or 0.125. Hence the new value of p in the next generation will be $\frac{0.5}{1-0.125} = 0.571$, and as $p+q=1$, the new value of $q=0.429$.*)

With each passing generation, at a similar selection pressure, it would be only a few years before the recessive allele declined, at a decreasing rate, to a very low level. For *Biston betularia* to have gone through the dramatic change it did, only a 25% selection pressure need in practice have applied. It is intriguing that a reversed selection in favour of the *typica* form is now occurring in the depolluted, smokeless zones of Manchester and Liverpool. Here then is micro-evolution, demonstrable and scientifically tested. So far as our own species is concerned there is no such neat example that we can point to of a single gene increasing in frequency as a result of selection. Many generations would be needed to detect such a change and we do not go to our doctors complaining of 'increased fitness'!

Table 3.1

	carbonaria	*typica*
Genotype	**AA** or **Aa**	**aa**
Phenotype	black	peppered grey
Released	601	201
Recaptured	205	34
% Recaptured	34.1	16.9
Relative fitness	1.00	0.50

*see Edwards K. J. R. *Evolution in Modern Biology* Arnold series 1977.

Table 3.2

Variety	carbonaria		typica
Genotype	AA	Aa	aa
Frequency before selection	p^2	$2pq$	q^2
Relative fitness	1.0	1.0	0.5
Frequency after selection	$p^2 \times 1$	$2pq \times 1$	$q^2 \times 0.5$

3.5 Heterozygous advantage

It will have been noted that in the last example the new mutant gene for melanism in the moth was dominant. Looking again at Figure 3.1, on the right-hand side, it will be apparent that if the new mutant is dominant to start with, where the gene frequency of A is quite low, the genotype frequency of the heterozygote Aa is rapidly rising. As the gene is expressed in the heterozygote to give black pigment, its adoption under selection will have been rapid. Looking at the left of Figure 3.1, imagine that a different new mutant **a** were to confer some advantage. It will not be expressed at all as a phenotype until its frequency rises sufficiently for **aa** genotypes to be formed. Thus recessive advantageous mutations will only slowly be picked up. This dominance advantage has enormous significance which is often unappreciated. As the dominance or expression of a gene is not always complete in a heterozygote, if a favoured gene is recessive but just lightly expressed in some of the heterozygotes then these individuals and these expressive genes will be selected. Often therefore there is a tendency for favoured genes to become dominant. Although dominance and Darwinian fitness are by no means the same, recessives are often found to be generally less beneficial and often harmful if rare. Where genes rival each other in fitness, heterozygosity is likely to prevail and both alleles may be expressed to some extent. Thus hybrids are known often to exhibit vigour and clearly individuals that are richly heterozygous have greater plasticity and survival chances as individuals and as members of a population. Perhaps the most striking example of **heterozygous advantage** in man is that of **sickle cell anaemia**, again a topic well covered by most genetics text books.

Table 3.3 summarises information on this human genetic condition. For areas of high sickle cell gene frequency such as West Africa, where 4% of the population may be born as anaemic sufferers, malaria is and has been for centuries a prevalent disease. In infection experiments Allison (1954) demonstrated the resistance to malaria of sickle cell trait and anaemic people. He was also able to observe the harsh and often lethal effects of this hereditary disease in the homozygous anaemic sufferers. By considering the blood

Table 3.3   Data on sickle cell anaemia

Genotype	Hb A/Hb A	Hb A/Hb S	Hb S/Hb S
Phenotype	normal	sickle cell trait	sickle cell anaemic
Blood Characteristics	normal	normal	anaemic
Malaria resistance	not resistant	resistant	resistant
Relative fitness	0.85	1.00	0.10
Relative abundance in high HbS incidence populations	$P^2=0.64$	$2pq=0.32$	$q^2=0.04$

characteristics and malarial resistance of the three phenotypes Allison (1961) was able to compute the relative fitness of the three genotypes. As shown in the table, relative to the heterozygote advantage, the homozygotes are both disadvantaged.

Where one or more alleles at a locus occur at a frequency above 1%, and hence cannot be reappearing by chance mutation alone but have some advantage in some circumstances, the species is said to be polymorphic. This **genetic polymorphism** increases the capacity of a species to exploit its environment, yet at the same time allows natural selection to stabilise a population without loss of variability. Man's genetic polymorphism today must reflect a past of equal variability in all hereditary characteristics.

3.6   The human mating system

Much of population genetics is based upon the assumption that mating between individuals is at random, indeed it is an assumption of the Hardy-Weinberg theorem. Is this true for our species? The 'Mendelian population' with its notion of a shared 'gene pool' is clearly rather indefinable but, within this group from which mates are selected by individuals, some **mating system** must operate. Human mating systems may well depart considerably from random breeding.

If mating is less than random, that is matings occur between close relatives more frequently than would occur by chance within their natural gene pool, it is termed **inbreeding**. The most extreme form of inbreeding in nature is self fertilisation in such organisms as self-pollinating plants. In such situations heterozygosity diminishes. Consider a species with genotype **Aa** which only self fertilises. On every recombination of gametes, offspring will be produced in the genotypes **AA**, **Aa** and **aa** in a ratio of 1:2:1. Only half will now be heterozygous and the heterozygosity will halve at each future generation. It is well known from genetical studies that inbreeding produces increased homozygosity and hence reduced variability and plasticity. In human evolution close inbreeding of small groups has obviously contributed to some distinguishing features of local populations. Very rarely has inbreeding been so close as to sanction brother-sister marriages, though this did occur in the royal households of the Ptolemies and the Incas.

In contrast to this, if mating is more than random, that is matings occur between close relatives less frequently than would occur by chance within their natural gene pool, it is termed **outbreeding**. Most sexually reproducing organisms have outbreeding mechanisms. Many mammals, for example, reared as young together have some sibling mating inhibitions. Almost all human societies have taboos about close inbreeding and often social customs and laws forbid marriage to close blood relatives. Clearly homozygosity for some recessive harmful alleles would be increased by such inter-marriage. Social customs promoting outbreeding are also encouraged; many African tribes, for example, have a requirement that wives come from a different clan within the tribe. Increased heterozygosity certainly increases variability and hence survival in a greater range of environments.

Other features of human mating maintain diversity in the population, thus favouring a variation of types in the human community. For example, in Britain there is apparently a positive tendency for people to seek marriage partners of matching status and intelligence, but a negative tendency for red-heads to marry red-heads. **Assortative mating**, as this phenomenon is called, can if positive, i.e. less than random, lead to class and caste systems, but these are unlikely to persist long enough to become genetic isolates.

The 'gene pool' is thus singularly indefinable for man. Each of us lives, as it were, in the centre of a series of concentric pools separated by barriers of social class, clan, tribe or race and geographical distance. Our culture encourages us to out-breed from our immediate area of the pool, but not to swim too far or leap over too many barriers. In that the human species is the widest pool of all, it should not surprise us that genetic variations will enter smaller more isolated Mendelian populations by the immigration of individuals with the genes they bear. Where two populations adjoin this is likely to be a reciprocal process. For example, between so-called 'whites' and 'blacks' there has been an obvious exchange of european or negroid external physical features. Yet many other genes are also involved. Thus the Duffy blood group genes, with a high frequency amongst Europeans and an almost complete absence from West Africans, occurs with a frequency of 11% in North American 'blacks'. Genes themselves can therefore migrate by adjacent gene pool jumping. Advantageous genes may therefore spread across a continent without actual human migration or conquest. Even if each man or woman in every generation only walked a few miles to find their spouse the advantageous genes they carried could circle the world in a hundred thousand years. Today the human gene pool is being stirred more than ever before.

3.7   Group selection

Early in this chapter evolutionary change by mutation and the selection of favoured individuals leading to changes in the gene frequency has been explained. The mating system operating within the gene pool further emphasises the freedom of individuals to produce genotype frequencies different from those predicted by random mating. It will be sufficiently clear that man is no ordinary animal for additionally, in a social species like ours, 'selection' may mean selection of societies rather than individuals alone.

Figure 3.2   A troop of baboons moving in open savannah; the organisation and behaviour of the troop as a whole will be a major factor in the survival of individual members (From Hall and de Vore, 1965.)

If a unit of animal society has a higher fitness than a competing social unit then clearly natural selection will operate in favour of that group. Not all members of the group need possess the favoured genes that confer the advantages nor need these advantages even be ones which are genetically determined. Perhaps the clearest example of **group selection** is that whereby the *altruism* or self-sacrificing behaviour of a mother towards its child may seemingly prejudice the mother's survival but increase the survival chances of the child which bears its mother's genes. This type of group selection is complex but clearly important in human evolution. The whole subject of **sociobiology** has grown up in the Neo-Darwinian paradigm to investigate this type of evolution and behaviour. The influence of this new discipline, pioneered by E. O. Wilson, will undoubtedly extend from biology into the social sciences.

3.8   Genetic drift

To this point genetic change has been considered as being subject to selection pressure alone. But the genetic equilibrium predicted by Hardy and Weinberg, and expressed by any vertical line in Figure 3.1, may actually move without any selection pressure at all for the fixed position of a genetic equilibrium (in the absence of migration, mutation and selection) only applies if the population is large. We know that in statistical theory small samples, for example less than fifty, are very 'unreliable', large samples being needed to reveal a true picture. In a similar way chance swings from one equilibrium position to another are far greater in a small population. Taking Figure 3.1 again, where a drawn vertical line represents an equilibrium, such a line is likely to shift to and fro quite markedly if the population is low. However, if the line drifts too far in either direction all of one kind of gene may be lost and the whole population will become 'fixed' as either homozygous for one allele or the other. **Sewall-Wright**, after whom this **genetic drift** effect is sometimes named, recognised its importance for evolution. In human evolution it may have had significance with small wandering or isolated bands which might have increased in homozygosity and lost variability. A **founder effect** of this sort may be recognised in some ethnic groups. All races, for example, have the ABO blood group genic system, but the frequencies of both A and B genes is very low amongst Central and South American Indian tribes. Total loss of genes A and B is illustrated by some South American tribes which have been shown to be entirely homozygous for the O group. Again, such a small population having passed through a gene-losing 'bottle-neck' may pick up entirely new features by mutation, which in the absence of competing alleles may give the new race a distinctive nature.

3.9 The origin of species

From what has been discussed in this chapter it will be clear that much evolutionary change is **phyletic**, a species changing greatly in the course of time, thus separating itself from its original ancestors. Were the ancestors and modern species to be brought together, we would say that they were indeed different species and would expect them to be either behaviourally incompatible (would you willingly marry a man-ape?) or genetically incompatible in chromosomal or allelic combinations.

However, at no time in phyletic evolution has a new species arisen as a distinct genetic event, so phyletic species must somehow be arbitrarily divided by horizontal divisions in time if they are to be discussed as different. S. J. Gould has recently pointed out (1977) that evolution may not proceed in a steady and slow advance but may do so in what appears from the fossil record to be a series of jumps. In his view long periods of equilibrium are punctuated by rapid change in form over a short period of time. Given the nature of inconstant environments in prehistory and yet obviously long periods of climatic stability in between, this view of sudden periods of phyletic change is not in conflict with older ideas of **phyletic gradualism**. We know from plant and animal breeding just how fast organisms can change under great selection pressures. Gould's **punctuated equilibrium** theory is not out of tune with Neo-Darwinism.

Phyletic evolution or **anagenesis** is in marked contrast to the formation of new species by diversification or **cladogenesis**. From what has been said about gene flow it will be clear that no speciation can occur without isolation for prolonged periods of time. That man today is one species, albeit of many races, is undoubted and attributable in large part to his migrations about the surface of the world over the past two million years, but early in human evolution diversification of hominid forms certainly occurred for we have the fossils to prove it. For this to have happened, we must postulate periods of isolation of an ecological or geographical nature so that upon their remeeting behavioural or genetic factors would have ensured an incompatibility in reproduction. Such incompatibility, once begun, is never broken down. A **species** is defined, by Mayr (1963), as 'a group of interbreeding natural populations, which are reproductively isolated from other such groups'. Isolation, originally a physical separation alone, becomes a genetic void. In evolution there is no going back.

This chapter has summarised the Neo-Darwinian view of the genetic basis for evolution and the origin of species. To close, one should clarify again the distinction which is made by biologists between past events of slow change in

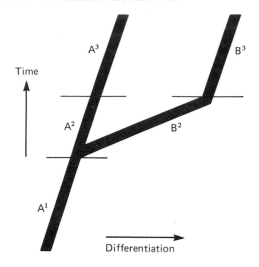

Figure 3.3   Two types of speciation

A^1, A^2, A^3 is a phyletic series of species which, with respect to time, arose in an anagenic manner. A^1, B^2, B^3 are a second phyletic series, but in that B^2 has changed more markedly in form than A^2, perhaps as a result of isolation, a branch has been produced. Such a branching-out origin of species is termed cladogenic.

A^3 and B^3 are contemporary species which, through their difference from each other, might be now genetically isolated if brought together in the same environment.

(See Figure 7.4 which deals with speciation patterns in man's ancestry.)

organic form, that is evolution, and the mechanism by which such changes may have taken place. That forms of life have changed over the length of geological time must be a fact, in the general sense of that word. But the historical fact of evolution can never have the same order of certainty as other presently verifiable facts in science, for we are barred by time from observing it and the process cannot be repeated! It is precisely for this reason that a Special Creation in 4004 BC cannot be disproved either. However, the hypotheses raised by the theory of evolution *are* able to be tested, at least in part as this chapter has aimed to show. It is because the theory of evolution by natural selection stands up so well to all attempts to prove it false that Neo-Darwinism becomes so strongly plausible and hence the probability, given the vast amount of evidence in its favour, of evolution being so likely as well. The trap that students of biology often fall into is to consider that because Neo-Darwinian theory *can* explain evolution it is automatically a complete explanation of it. This would be faulty logic. On the one hand many biologists feel that when our understanding of the complexity of the selection process and the intricacy of the genetic system is complete natural selection will still be seen to be the major or even sole mechanism. But others, while acknowledging that natural selection is important feel that it is not the sole mechanism that has given rise to such a diverse organic world. We need to accept both these scientific views as we must also accept the Creationist view, however implausible that may seem.

4 The primates: ancestors and contemporary cousins

4.1 Introduction

At the termination of the great age of dinosaurs 70 million years ago, not only were the great reptiles giving way to a diversity of birds and early mammals, but a substantial change was also taking place in plant evolution. Plant and animal communities interact in a complex way. What seems to have occurred was a retreat by the scaly resinous conifers before the new diversity of flowering plants whose growth and decay had a more rapid turn over and whose strategy for reproduction involved animal vectors for their pollen, fruits and seeds. We shall never fully know what life was like in the early Palaeocene, but the modern tropical forest was created at that time, and one group of shrew-like placental mammals secured niches for themselves in the colourful three-dimensional world of trees, branches, leaves, flowers and fruits high above the ground.

The members of the **Order of Primates** are anatomically primitive, for in common with the simplest terrestrial mammals, they have few of the specialised physical adaptations of the wide divergence of mammalian types. The specialised features that they do have are all related, directly or indirectly, to **arboreal life**. The Primates today consist of approximately 150 species, most but not all of which a layman would describe quite correctly as monkeys. Almost all of them are arboreal, grasping the branches with hands and even their feet, though some larger species spend much time on the ground. They have keen eyesight, and their vision is directed forward from foreshortened faces. They hold their heads erect and often sit or move about with bodies upright rather than horizontal. Some few are nocturnal, but most are active by day. They live in family or larger social groups of mixed ages and sexes. They are opportunistic feeders, mostly on plant material such as leaves, stems, flowers, fruits and seeds but some may feed on captured animal prey. The higher members of the Order exhibit a dexterity, visual perception, intelligence, social organisation and consciousness of themselves and their environment without parallel in the animal kingdom. As *you* are probably sitting upright, turning the pages of this book with your modified forelimbs and making conscious appreciation of visual information in a rapid manner, and as you probably score on all the other criteria mentioned above you must include yourself in the Order of Primates.

Figure 4.1 sets out the taxonomic groupings of a range of representative species of living primates some of which are illustrated in Figure 4.2. Before reviewing some primate examples the nature of the subdivisions of the Order itself must be appreciated. Linnaeus constructed his classification scheme on an hierarchical basis. Any group of organisms is described by its common characteristics and named as a particular *taxon*. The highest taxa or groupings encompass a great range of forms with few common characteristics; the lowest commonly used taxon is the species, the members of which are clearly similar by virtue of their common gene pool. In its classic form the system is hierarchically based as follows:

fewer common characteristics   KINGDOM   larger groupings
                                PHYLUM
                                CLASS
                                ORDER
                                FAMILY
                                GENUS
more common characteristics   SPECIES   smaller groupings

Because at times there may be several natural groupings in the next hierarchical assemblage above, whose group affinities would be clearer by further separation, more horizontal divisions can be made. As there are ten peculiarly distinct families of primates in this Order the hierarchy has been further divided here to descend:

ORDER
Sub-Order
Infra Order
Super Family
FAMILY

4.2 Prosimians

The primates are divided into the man-like apes and monkeys, the anthropoids, and more primitive **prosimians** (literally 'before the monkeys'). The **tarsier** of Indonesia, *Tarsius*, is a useful model for an archetypal primate. The short nose, large eyes and prominent ears are striking features; long flexible fingers have tiny pads and nail-like claws. Its teeth are well adapted for insect eating, the insects being captured by leaps from a vertical clinging position on a plant stem. For a mammal only 12 cm long in the body its brain is both large and complex. Its single young, in which great care is invested, is carried clinging to its mother's belly fur.

The **lorisids** contain a similarly nocturnal and leaping form in the bush-baby of Africa. *Galago* is larger than the tarsier and more catholic in its diet. Although hand-over-hand creeping on all four limbs is its normal locomotion pattern the bush-baby is capable of rapidly repeated leaps of several metres with an accuracy and coordination demanding in brain control. Other lorisids, such as the potto, are slower moving and feed on fruit or hunt for roosting birds.

The **lemuroids** are an exciting relict of the past. Fossil lemurs are known from North America and Europe and can be presumed to have been widespread but inferior competitors to the later apes and monkeys. Today they are only found on the island of Madagascar, as eighteen diverse species, completely isolated from competition with other primates by the surrounding Indian Ocean. Being largely diurnal, these seemingly cat-like prosimians live in large social groups. Their young grow up within a troop and much time is spent in learning the skills of life. Social group structures allow this extended

ORDER	SUB-ORDER	INFRA-ORDER	SUPER-FAMILY	FAMILY	GENUS	SPECIES	COMMON ENGLISH NAME
PRIMATES	PROSIMII	TARSIFORMES	TARSIOIDEA	TARSIIDAE	Tarsius	spectrum	Tarsier
		LORISIFORMES	LORISOIDEA	LORISIDAE	Loris	tardigradus	Loris
					Perodicticus	potto	Potto
					Galago	senegalensis	Bush-baby
		LEMURIFORMES	LEMUROIDEA	LEMURIDAE	Lemur	catta	Ring-tail Lemur
				INDRIDAE	Indri	indri	Indri
					Propithecus	verrauxi	Sifaka
ANTHROPOIDEA	PLATYRRHINI New World Monkeys		CEBOIDEA	CALLITRICHIDAE	Callithrix	jacchus	Marmoset
				CEBIDAE	Allouata	caraya	Howler Monkey
					Cebus	capuchinus	Capuchin
					Ateles	ater	Spider Monkey
	CATARRHINI Old World Monkeys		CERCOPITHECOIDEA	COLOBINAE	Presbytis	entellus	Langur
					Colobus	guereza	Colobus
				CERCOPITHECIDAE	Macaca	sylvanus	Barbary Ape
					Macaca	mulatta	Rhesus Monkey
					Macaca	fuscata	Japanese Macaque
					Papio	anubis	Olive Baboon
					Papio	hamadryas	Hamadryas Baboon
					Theropithecus	gelada	Gelada Baboon
					Cercopithecus	aethiops	Guenon
					Erythrocebus	patas	Patas Monkey
	HOMINOIDEA			HYLOBATINAE	Hylobates	lar	Gibbon
					Symphalangus	syndactylus	Siamang
				PONGIDAE	Pongo	pygmaeus	Orangutan
					Pan	troglodytes	Chimpanzee
					Gorilla	gorilla	Gorilla
				HOMINIDAE	Homo	sapiens	Modern Man

Figure 4.1   The classification of man amongst the Primates

Figure 4.2   Representative species of Primate showing the range of form and locomotor patterns in the Order

(a) *Colobus*   semi-brachiation (Old World)
(b) *Potto*   slow climbing
(c) *Ateles* (spider monkey)   semi-brachiation (New World)
(d) *Hylobates* (gibbon)   brachiation
(e) *Microcebus* (mouse lemur)   quadrupedal branch running
(f) *Pongo* (orangutan)   quadrumanous climbing
(g) *Papio* (baboon)   quadrupedal walking
(h) *Gorilla*   quadrupedal knuckle walking
(i) *Tarsier*   vertical clinger and leaper
(j) *Homo*   bipedal walker with freed forelimbs

26

development time and the group's cooperation in feeding and evading predators confers a greater survival on the cooperating members. None of the lemuroids have the degree of manual dexterity of the monkeys and apes, or even their intelligence, but they do display an early evolution of social grouping in the primates.

4.3 New World monkeys

At some time in the Eocene about 50 million years ago when the lemuroids were widespread across the then tropical North America and Europe, it is believed that the tectonic rifting between Greenland and Spitzbergen isolated 'New World' North America from Eurasia. It is hard to conceive of these drifting continents, for which there is now good geological evidence, but a group of North American lemuroids is believed to have given rise to the **platyrrhine ceboid** monkeys. How the **New World monkeys** reached the then isolated continent of South America we shall never fully know, but it is clear that the lemurs of North America died out and that the ceboids, who share the same primitive dental formula as the lemurs, expanded and radiated to fill all the forest niches of the great South and Central American forests.

The diminutive **callitrichid** marmosets and tamarins have evolved an almost squirrel-like form with claws instead of nails. The larger **cebids** such as the spider monkey have amazingly prehensile tails as a diagnostic Family feature. In many ways the cebids have converged in form and behaviour with the cercopithecoid monkeys and hylobatid gibbons whose origins have been entirely different.

4.4 Old World monkeys

The **catarrhine** primates are most simply divided into the **Old World monkeys**, the apes, and men. The sequence of evolutionary change giving rise to these groups is still far from clear but it is sufficient to say that there is a good succession of fossils from lemuroid to ape-like forms, lacking tails, and much evidence to suggest that many Old World monkey species such as those in the *Cercopithecus* genus are relatively recent. Put simply, monkeys did not give rise to apes nor indeed, as we shall see, did apes as we know them today give rise to mankind.

Most of the **cercopithecids** are too familiar to justify full description here: the rhesus monkey commonly used as a research animal, the Japanese macaques that range from the snowline to the seashore, the African baboons of the savannah are all familiar to us from film or from visits to zoos. The **colobine** sub-family are an exclusively herbivorous group, with a well-developed caecal fermentation chamber comparable to that found in other herbivorous non-ruminant mammals. These are high forest canopy dwellers. Amongst the more typical cercopithecids, the baboons and patas monkey are particularly interesting to students of human evolution as they have largely taken to savannah living outside the protection of the forest as the primitive hominids also seem to have done.

4.5 Hominoids

Far closer to ourselves in body form are the **gibbons** and **great apes** (**pongids**). The gibbons' beautiful arm-swinging locomotion through the forest canopy is a distinctive arboreal adaptation. On the ground, out of their element, they have an intriguingly human upright walking waddle. The **brachiation** or arm swinging and this occasional **bipedalism** in the gibbons differs from movement patterns in the three great apes. The orangutan, *Pongo*, is seemingly four armed and can achieve almost any contortion up a tree. The adults are too heavy to brachiate but this behaviour is seen in more frisky juveniles. The chimpanzee, *Pan*, and the largest of all apes, *Gorilla*, are similarly too heavy for a fully arboreal existence. Chimpanzees are the more arboreal of the two, but both spend most of their time on the ground and walk **quadrupedally** on their knuckles rather than upon open hands as the monkeys do. These **hominoids** are so intricately bound up with human origins that they will be reviewed more fully in Chapter 6. These living **pongids** are so tantalizingly man-like and yet so vastly different that we must tread carefully in defining their distinctive characteristics and, in comparison, our own. What is clear is that they, like us, have gone through a long history of **arboreal adaptation**.

4.6 The characteristic features of the primates

From this necessarily brief introduction to the primates it is possible to enumerate some nine biological features of importance which owe their origins to arboreal living or forest life and which have produced a mosaic of features from which man has emerged.

1. The grasping limb

The hands and often the feet of primates are modified for grasping with their elongated and highly mobile digits. The innermost digit of the forelimb, the **pollex** or thumb, opposes the other four digits. In the hind limb it is general for the first digit, the **hallux** to be opposable, though it is not in man. Claws are found primitively, but all primates have some flattened nails (most have them exclusively) that provide support for the pads of sensitive skin on the palmar (hand palm) or plantar (foot sole) surfaces. The pads have ridge patterns or **dermatoglyphs** (finger prints), the slight deformations of which convey detailed sensory information to the brain.

2. The exploratory forelimb

Arboreal grasping and arm rotation give the forearm a far greater mobility. The freedom of the proximal end of the radius to rotate, and hence allow twisting of the forearm, enables the hand to be flat on the ground (**pronate**) or upturned (**supinate**). The tactile sensitivity of the palmar surface makes the arm an exteroceptive sense organ able to test the environment as well as to transfer food to the mouth or to hold objects for closer examination by eye, nose and ear. We take this so much for granted in ourselves; perhaps by saying that in this respect our arms are analogous to the elephant's trunk the extent of the modification can be appreciated.

3. A generalised herbivorous digestive system

Early primates may well have been insectivorous for all families have still got some omnivorous members, but generally the primates have diversified into herbivorous niches. Primitive mammals have cutting cheek teeth with three cusps suitable for crunching up insects. The primates have developed an extra cusp on their molars making them **quadritubercular**, more block-like and thus effective at crunching vegetable matter. The premolars have become more molar-like. All Old World catarrhines have a $\frac{2}{2}:\frac{1}{1}:\frac{2}{2}:\frac{3}{3}$ **dental formula**. The colon is enlarged and the caecum an active fermentation chamber.

4. A reduction in the olfactory sense

Scent trailing is impossible through the canopies of trees and primates have a reduced sense of smell compared to most other mammals. Their organs of olfaction are atrophied; noses are shorter and only some prosimians have a glandular sensitive end to the muzzle. All of the anthropoids lack this dog-like 'wet nose' and have developed an undivided large upper lip whose function in feeding and vocalisation is clearly important. This upper lip size and mobility gives the anthropoids their more human face, and the use of these lips in much territorial hooting and calling has replaced the scent marking of territory that characterises many terrestrial mammals with a more developed 'nose'.

5. Keen and stereoscopic vision

Leaping and accurate grasping requires not only detailed vision but rapid accommodation and stereoscopy. Primates have large, relatively well-developed eyes. Although the nocturnal primates have exclusively monochrome rod vision, colour cone vision is found in all diurnal species with much the same retinal distribution pattern as in man. The one-to-one relationship of cones to nerve cells ensures acuity. The optical axes of the eyes are parallel and gather from the same visual field. Both sides of the brain receive fibres from both eyes, enabling visual depth to be perceived by the brain.

6. Large brains

Skulls of fossil lemurs show that early in the evolution of forest-dwelling primates, brains expanded greatly in comparison to those of insectivore mammals. The hindmost occipital lobe of the cerebral hemispheres is greatly enlarged. This is the centre for visual imaging and interpretation. Sensory and motor cortical areas are also expanded and more deeply fissured to provide more grey matter by brain cortex folding. The locomotor coordination centres of the cerebellum are also expanded. In higher primates the temporal lobes associated with sound discrimination are enlarged markedly as well. Life in the trees clearly puts a premium on brain fitness. The grace and precision of a monkey moving at speed through a forest canopy or the split second timing and poise of a gymnast are achievements of a highly developed brain.

7. Modified skulls

A more generally **upright posture** in a resting squatting position but with a forward-looking face necessitates two changes of skull form. First, the occipital condyles, on which the atlas vertebra of the neck articulates, must come more under the head's centre of gravity. A backwardly expanding cerebrum and cerebellum have led to a declined emergent angle of the medulla oblongata and spinal cord from its previous posterior direction. The **foramen magnum**, or hole through which the medulla emerges, is thus more posterio-ventral in the primates and in man right below the cranium itself. Secondly, reduction of the nose and muzzle has shortened the face. This has led to a backward movement of the jaws in the absence of muzzle support, to bring them more fully under the cranium. A third feature of all primate skulls relates to the orbits, for the enlarged and forward-facing eyes. A post-orbital bar, a pillar of bone, is formed behind the eye socket whilst brow ridges above support and protect the eye.

8.   Reduced number of offspring and intensive infant care

For life in the trees, a bird's reproductive strategy is to make a nest, lay eggs and rear nestlings. Predation risks are high but persistence and secretive behaviour ensure survival. Amongst arboreal mammals squirrels have followed this type of nesting pattern but bats and most primates have adopted a way of life in which few young are produced at each birth, and these cling to the mother's body and only slowly gain independence. Primates are unusual amongst mammals for their low foetus number, relatively long gestation period for their size and long infant–mother relationship. Infants are carried from birth and suckled by the mother on two pectoral mammae. Because behaviour based on learning is paramount for success, primates are not hurried through their childhood. Here is a unique primate feature of increased reproductive fitness by decreased litter size. The consequences of this in human evolution have been profound.

9.   The support of a society

Primates, especially the higher ones, lead markedly unsolitary lives. Most individuals are bonded at least loosely, for long periods to mates, dependants or parents in family groups or larger troops. Living in such groups, the discovery of widely-dispersed yet localised concentrations of food, such as a fruiting tree, is easier and more efficient. Mutual defence against predators is more effective, with the troop's numerous ears and eyes, and this corporate protection activity reinforces group cohesion. Lengthy rearing of young confers an adaptive advantage on the individual but in its dependancy period the juvenile and its mother need the troop's support. The dependancy of the young upon the troop is reciprocated, for the troop depends for its success upon the help of new young recruits. This **social interdependancy**, arguably the most advanced primate characteristic, is the basis of our own human society.

5 Palaeoanthropology

5.1 Introduction

The fossil evidence for human origins has accumulated at an increasing pace over the past hundred years. **Palaeontology**, the study of fossils, is a well-developed science, but in the study of fossil man the techniques and refinement of method have reached considerable sophistication for human fossils are few and fragmentary and interpretation is all important. This chapter concerns the methods of the **palaeoanthropologist**.

Discovery, excavation, dating, reconstructing, cataloguing, interpreting and naming are the main problems to be faced. What is now the work of teams was once the province of individualist fossil collectors, such as Eugene Dubois, Robert Broom, Raymond Dart and Louis Leakey, and the kind of rivalry that such individualism engendered lives on with the research teams of today.

5.2 Fossilisation

How remains come to be fossilised at all and the circumstances surrounding the process is one of the new fields in palaeontology. It is called **taphonomy**. Much depends upon the events surrounding the death of the animal. Dismemberment by carnivores and scavengers, for example, may scatter bones widely from each other; chewing may scratch or pierce the bones; weathering agents such as heat, frost, wind and acid water may decay bones rapidly. Taphonomic studies of what happens to animal corpses in the wild have helped greatly in interpreting fossil remains. What is quite clear is that rapid burial in lake sediments, in pools of mud or under volcanic ash falls is most likely to produce complete fossil individuals. Such events are extremely unlikely but they have happened and have given us very complete skeletal collections. More commonly only tantalisingly small fragments are found in geological deposits. Teeth have a special importance in palaeontology because of their great hardness and hence permanence as fossils.

Once surrounded by fine soil particles, buried bones will be subject to various processes most of which will lead to decay. Bone, by dry weight, is 35% protein and 65% mineral. The protein slowly degenerates, giving an index as it does so of the bone's age, but in the absence of dissolving acids, other minerals in the medium may move into the bone structure. In basic sediments or lavas the calcium content of the bone mineral, hydroxy-apatite, may be added to, or, by molecular substitution, it may be replaced entirely by substances such as silica. A typical mineralised fossil is thus a heavier but exact replica of the originally buried bone. Occasionally the massive weight of strata may greatly distort or crush a fossil, or shearing forces may distort it slightly.

Caves in limestone provide excellent fossilisation sites, for the litter of bones from human or carnivore occupation are sequentially bedded down in a suitable environment for mineralisation. The advent of ritual burial in man, beginning perhaps 50 000 years ago, has been of enormous value to archaeology.

The **soft parts** of early man are unknown as fossils. Complete preservation of human flesh by mummification and dehydration has occurred in Egyptian tombs and a comparable wet anaerobic acid preservation is known from certain Danish peat bogs. Both of these forms of preservation enable us to see all of the facial features of people dead some thousands of years. However, it is too much to hope that such climatic constancy as these conditions require would apply for as much as a million years, so all flesh, skin and facial shapes ascribed to early man are based on plausible reconstruction alone.

5.3 Traces and artefacts

Other remains and traces may be important too. First, footprints of early hominids are known from 3.7 Ma (millions of years ago). **Artefacts**, objects fashioned by man, such as stone tools and pottery, also add enormously to the evidences of man's early existence. Indeed as man becomes increasingly modern in fossil form, these artefacts become increasingly significant in interpreting **cultural evolution**. Intensive study of 'living sites', where communities once left their tools and refuse behind, reveals not only the secrets of the tool manufacture, but also the use to which they were put, such as cutting meat from bones or hammering them open to obtain the marrow. Such traces and artefacts need to be added to the fossil evidences with which they are contemporary.

5.4 The excavation of deposits

With respect to human evolution Asia and Africa have the most important deep deposits of sedimentary beds, spanning long periods of the Pliocene and Pleistocene eras. The **Great Rift Valley** of Africa is the most outstanding single location for fossils of early man anywhere in the world. The series of faults and diverging and converging valleys and rift walls runs for three thousand miles, from the Red Sea to Southern Africa. For many millions of years the down faulting and upward movements have continued. Volcanoes have come and gone. Rift bottom lakes have formed and drained many times and expanded and contracted in extent with the changing seasons and climatic periods. Volcanic ash, lava flows of basalt or lava conglomerates sandwich the lake bed sediments in the rock strata. Here evidence of more than four million years of human evolution is interred, although only a fraction of the evidence has been unearthed and a minute amount described.

The erosion, by wind and rain, of these bedded fossils from their strata re-exposes them to the air and probable final decay, but because of their hardness they tend to accumulate at the bottom of eroded slopes. This is where the palaeontologist often first finds them and excavations begin. A new **fossil site** is first mapped fully and reference to local features of topography and geology noted, for nearby volcanic beds may be used for absolute dating. After mapping, the surface fossils are picked up, and then on a grid system the most promising areas of the site are excavated away in a series of blocks or

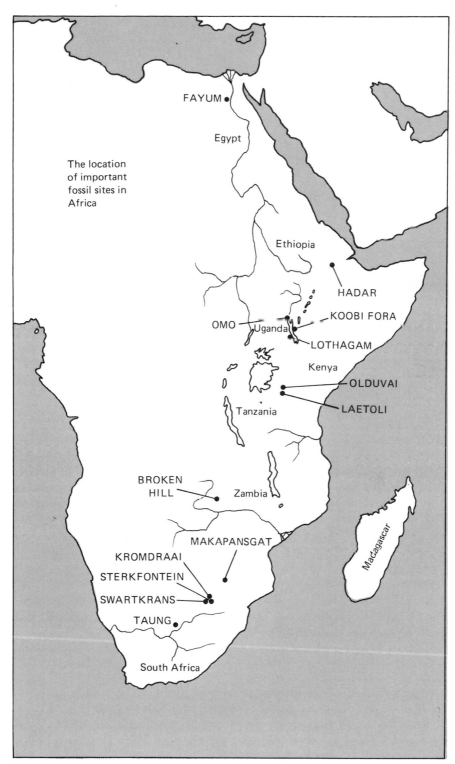

The location
of important
fossil sites in
Africa

FAYUM ●

Egypt

Ethiopia

● HADAR

OMO
Uganda
KOOBI FORA

LOTHAGAM

Kenya

OLDUVAI

LAETOLI

Tanzania

BROKEN
HILL
Zambia

Madagascar

MAKAPANSGAT

KROMDRAAI
STERKFONTEIN
SWARTKRANS

TAUNG ●

South Africa

Figure 5.1

trenches, down one layer at a time in the bedded plane. Fossil finds are mapped as they appear and in the process a three-dimensional record emerges. Fine soil may be sifted for small teeth or flakes of bone and large fossils may be strengthened with acrylic hardeners, or if very delicate, cased in plaster for removal to the laboratory. Specimens are then numbered, cleaned with meticulous care, using fine dental picks and scrapers, and then put aside for full cataloguing.

5.5   Dating fossils

The dating of fossils and their sites is an essential part of the palaeontologist's fieldwork. **Geochronology**, the science of rock age estimation, is particularly important in palaeoanthropology because the time sequencing of fossil forms greatly affects one's interpretation of them. 'Once bitten, twice shy' has been the motto of every worker in this field since the perpetration of the Piltdown Man hoax, in 1912, in which an ape jaw and human skull were cunningly placed in a Sussex fossil collector's way in order that the discovery might discredit a rival palaeontologist at the British Museum. Indeed so vexed is the question of dating that it still manifestly affects people's judgement of what they are handling. This is perhaps the best reason for adopting the **cladistic approach** to fossil man used by Colin Patterson, at the British Museum, whose predecessors were so cruelly deceived by the Piltdown forgery.

In the dating of fossils, the find should be first established as contemporary with its bedded horizon. This is often not simple to establish, but the bones of one horizon should be chemically alike in composition. Fossils may be washed out of higher horizons and rebedded into the lower ones and hence appear older than they really are. Once the authenticity of the bedding is established, two types of dating are possible, **relative dating** and **absolute dating**. Relative dating cross connects one stratum in one area to other strata elsewhere, for the fauna at one time would have been widespread and the same species are often fossilised many miles away. For example, in the Great Rift, wild pig fossils are vastly more abundant than those of early man. Of the several species found, all were evolving slowly and make a reliable reference point for the relative ages of sites. A second relative dating method employs the fact that cooling lavas of the volcanic beds take on the prevailing magnetic polarity of the earth when they solidify. The earth's magnetic field is not fixed but may 'flip over' and reverse the north and south magnetic poles. Such major and minor reversals are recorded with great relative consistency over the entire history of the earth and are providing an increasingly reliable time scale.

Absolute dating depends on the decremental decay rate of radioactive isotopes in organic or volcanic materials. This decay is independent of temperature and pressure and prevailing chemical conditions and is a truly accurate clock provided that measurements are made on good materials with the right techniques. The **radiocarbon dating** (^{14}C) method (half-life 5.7×10^3 a) is most useful for the span of recent prehistory and will date any **organic material** back to 40 000 years ago. The **potassium argon dating** (^{40}K–^{40}Ar) method (half-life 1.3×10^9 a) only has a useful accuracy with material more than half a million years old. Its absolute reliability is perhaps only ± 0.2 Ma

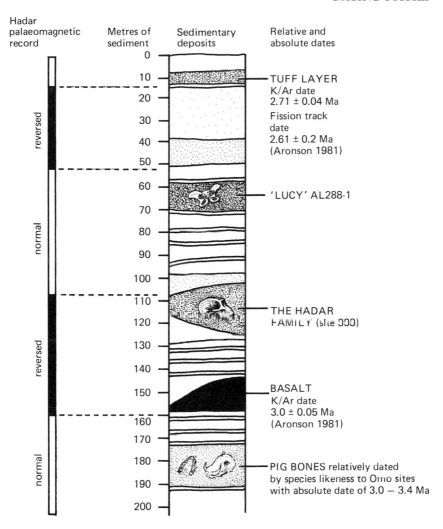

Figure 5.2 Relative and absolute dating of fossil deposits

although readings are consistent to the nearest 50 000 years. Potassium-argon dating can only be done on volcanic material in which the potassium isotope's extent of decay, from the date of solidification, can be monitored. **Fission track dating** methods now seem to be the most reliable for any fossils found in association with contemporary volcanic deposits over 10 000 years old. In this technique, rather than monitoring the radioactive decay rate, the **fission tracks** produced by nuclear explosions in volcanic glass, or crystals of zirconium, are revealed by etching and are then counted. Such nuclear physics technology has put an absolute date in millions of years on what were formerly only estimates of age.

A concordance of different dating methods is preferred if ages are to be believed. Figure 5.2 shows how dates for one important site at Hadar, in Ethiopia, are given. The implied accuracy of the dates may be misleading. All we can certainly conclude is that this bedded sequence of 200 metres of deposits spans a period of time of about a million years duration, beginning slightly more than three million years ago. Dates need also to be rechecked carefully if they are at all unusual. For example, a specimen of *Homo habilis*, ER 1470, discovered by Richard Leakey, and dated initially as 2.6 Ma has had to be redesignated to 1.9 Ma after more careful tests (1980). This is unfortunate too, for this notable find has been described in the context of the older date in Leakey's excellent *Origins* (1977). Geologists are thus shy of absolute dates; relative dating can be more finely discriminating in 'reading the rocks'.

5.6   Interpretation of remains

The analysis of fossil collections is exacting work. Out of the discipline, however, may come great discoveries especially now that computerised data banks and searches are possible. David Pilbeam uses the following (here much simplified) data retrieval system on *Ramapithecus* sites in Pakistan. For each fossil the following is data banked:

1   An alphabetical letter code and number (e.g. Johanson's 'Lucy' is AL 288–1, Richard Leakey's famous *Homo habilis* skull is KNM-ER-1470).
2   Assignation to the lowest taxonomic position, down towards species level, that can be given with confidence and full classification above this level (e.g. Primate; Anthropoidea; Hominoidea; Ramapithecidae).
3   Anatomical nature together with condition and degree of wear (e.g. left humerus, upper half only).
4   Locality number (e.g. site 333 at Hadar); site location and bedded position.
5   Taphonomic indicators: abrasion, weathering, toothmarks, bone fractures, evidence of disease etc.
6   The size measurements of specimen; relevant mean size measurements for the taxon.

Such data storage makes searches for comparable material easier and also allows for statistical analysis of many different specimens. **Multivariate analysis** of such large amounts of data enables generalisations to be made in the discussion and interpretation of results.

Many challenges may then follow. Reconstructed crania may have their volume measured as an estimate of brain capacity. Plaster of Paris casts may be made of important fossils and sent to other workers. In seeking dietary clues stereoscan microscopy may be used to study the micro-wear on teeth. An overall view of the range of other animals on a site beside the hominid ones may give indications of the kind of environment in which they all lived and to which they were adapted. For many sites in Pleistocene Europe fossil pollen has been analysed and used to highlight major climatic changes.

During the African Pleistocene wet and dry periods, the **pluvials** and **inter-pluvials**, alternated much as the **ice ages** and **interglacial periods** alternated in Europe. What the reasons for these great climatic shifts were or how the pluvial periods related to the ice ages is still not clear, but they would have greatly altered the local environment. Rather than adapt *in situ* to such changes, we know that most plant and animal communities slowly shifted to and fro across the continents. It must have been in this great diversity of habitats, climates and mammalian forms that much of human evolution occurred. These ideas capture our imagination but it has been the painstaking work of palaeontologists that has given us this perspective.

5.7   Naming fossils

The naming of hominid fossils has been as confusing to the student of evolution as it has been a subject of contention amongst the palaeoanthropologists themselves. An index of **nomenclature** and **synonyms** is given in Appendix I. As we have seen, the discoverer of a fossil tries to place it in the lowest taxon into which it will fit. If it is outside the parameters of known fossils in its range of characters, it may be described as a new species or even genus if specific status alone seems insufficient to do justice to the specimen's uniqueness. Two factors have encouraged a plethora of namings. First, there has been a dearth of fossils to create that breadth of variation we now accept for any species; each find has seemed unique. Secondly, discoverers feel so proud of their fossil novelty that new names feel at the time only justly deserved! Certainly the media respond to new names and from the publicity new research funds flow to make further field work possible. Two factors work conservatively against these **splitters**. The rule of priority, in nomenclature, dictates that once a type specimen is described any subsequent namings that prove to be in the taxon must conform, unless agreed by convention to be distinctly different. Thus Dubois' named discovery of *Pithecanthropus erectus* in 1891 was later recognised to be in the same genus as ourselves, *Homo* (named by Linnaeus). Thus *Pithecanthropus* disappeared into the genus *Homo*, and *Homo erectus* became its species. Similarly the genus *Australopithecus* has taken in *Zinjanthropus*, *Plesianthropus* and *Paranthropus*. Within the genera there are inevitable arguments over species naming, especially in the plausibly phyletic lines of *Australopithecus* and *Homo*. The second factor in favour of the **lumpers**, who like to have taxa comprising greater variability, is that it does enable discussion to continue without scientists overdefending previously held positions.

Throughout this book the term 'man' is used in a generic sense, without a capital letter, as the common name in English for our species.

The naming of archaeological periods, and cultures, and events with geological periods is again complex. The **Günz**, **Mindel**, **Riss** and **Würm** are the Pleistocene ice ages of Europe which span the last million years. As it is only 20 000 years since the last one ended there is no great reason to think that we are in anything more than an interglacial period at present. The terms **Palaeolithic**, **Mesolithic** and **Neolithic** mean ancient, middle and the new Stone Ages respectively. The Neolithic is marked by stone age agriculture, the Mesolithic is a relatively short period before it. The Palaeolithic extends from the early origins of our genus, *Homo*, right up to the fully modern European cavemen of the last ice age. As these are cultural designations alone, it will be recognised that for some primitive peoples the Palaeolithic has effectively continued to the present day.

6   Descent from the trees

The most significant feature of early hominid evolution, indeed the feature which has seemed to pre-adapt hominids for further evolution in the human direction, was upright walking. Some remarkable fossil footprints from Laetoli, in Tanzania, dated at 3.6 Ma show that this feature was indeed developed early, two million years before any stone tool making evidence is to be found. Upright walking, bipedalism, is not an appropriate means of locomotion for a tree dwelling primate and one of the puzzles of early human evolution has been to see how such a transformation occurred.

There are numerous fossil primates known, from the Palaeocene to the Pleistocene, which can be compared to the living forms. Elwyn Simons (1972) gives the classification of some 360 species of primate, more than half of which are extinct and most only known from very rudimentary remains. Although we cannot trace a direct line of ancestry, we can pick species from along the way and say that they were close to the actual line of human descent; they have an **ancestor dependent relationship**.

6.1   Origin of the anthropoids

The story starts 60 million years ago. *Plesiadapis*, an abundant fossil form from the **Palaeocene** forests, was a long-tailed prosimian perhaps not unlike a large grey squirrel in appearance. From well preserved limb bones it is possible to see how it was an efficient arboreal leaper. In the **Eocene**, the first vertical clingers and leapers appear. One such is *Necrolemur*, known from a dozen skulls and some limb bones showing tibio-fibial fusion. The short face, large orbits and hind limb rigidity indicate a bush-baby type of prosimian. At the close of the Eocene amongst the primates there are as yet neither apes nor monkeys in the fossil record, but the **Oligocene** sees the beginning of this classificatory division and the origins of the Anthropoidea. Not far from Cairo is the Egyptian fossil site of Fayum. Between 40 and 25 million years ago this now desert area was a dense tropical rain forest lining the banks of a broad sluggish river. In this river's deposits many significant early primate remains are to be found.

Table 4   Numbers of living and extinct primate species

	Living	Extinct	Total
Genera	52	96	148
Species	154	206	360

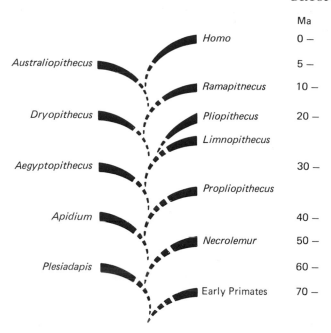

Figure 6.1 A phylogenetic tree to illustrate the ancestor dependant relationship of man with the various fossil primates that fit closest to the human branch

Apidium was an abundant arboreal squirrel–monkey like form, probably a high canopy dweller. It shows a kinship in tooth structure to some of the early arboreal apes of 10 million years later, but for other anatomical reasons it stands at the parting of the ways between Old World, catarrhine, and New World, platyrrhine forms. By 30 Ma, in the **Oligocene**, the diversity of present Old World apes was beginning. *Propliopithecus* is one of several lightly built early forms. It could arguably be ancestral to the modern gibbons, though it probably had a tail and behaved in a more spider-monkey like manner. It does however have dental features more like the early man-like apes or hominids. The almost contemporary *Aegyptopithecus* is a larger ape but still only of gibbon size. This was probably an agile generalised rain forest dweller adapted to a leaf- and fruit-eating diet. Virtually complete skulls of this animal are known from the Fayum forest beds. *Aegyptopithecus* was clearly a fore-runner of the dryopithecine apes of the Miocene and as these lead directly on to the chimpanzee, it must clearly be close to the human ancestral line from which the hominids arose. It was, however, a relatively small-brained creature and we can only guess that it was still light enough to leap and brachiate, though it may well have come occasionally to the ground.

6.2 *Dryopithecus*

The fossil story now shifts from Fayum to other fossil-rich localities. In the Miocene beds of East Africa and Europe, the ape line seems to radiate out further. Two possible gibbon ancestors *Limnopithecus* and *Pliopithecus* are found, whilst contemporary with them a great radiation of chimpanzee-like

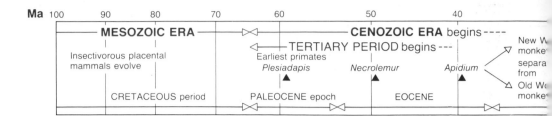

Ma 100   90   80   70   60   50   40

| MESOZOIC ERA | ⋈ | CENOZOIC ERA begins ---- |

New W monke⋅

TERTIARY PERIOD begins ---

Insectivorous placental mammals evolve

Earliest primates
Plesiadapis ▲   *Necrolemur* ▲   *Apidium* ▲

separa from

CRETACEOUS period   PALEOCENE epoch   EOCENE

Old We monke⋅

▲ date of fossil find

dryopithecine apes occurred. *Dryopithecus* is known from wide areas of Europe and Africa. Their chimpanzee-like nature was recognised in the last century; even the generic naming of the East African dryopithecines as *Proconsul* was in honour of Consul, a famous Manchester Zoo chimp who endeared himself to the late Victorians. These apes, which turn up in numerous fossil beds, were clearly abundant and undoubtedly successful forest dwellers. Though lighter boned than the chimpanzee they probably progressed on the ground as **knuckle walkers**. It is hard for us to imagine the great Miocene forests of Europe but they must have been alive with the calls of these undoubtedly vociferous and social primates as they moved in troops looking for fruiting trees. Ranging in weight from 15 to 30 kg they could still have been light enough to climb and swing well even if they did not brachiate as freely as the gibbons. Their dentition was almost identical to that of the modern African apes, having a U-shaped dental arcade, large canines and teeth with thin dental enamel. This would have suited them for a soft fruit or leaf eating diet in the forest environment much like that of their present day pongid descendants in Africa. The anatomically largest dryopithecine fossils, of *D. major*, come from volcanic ash beds on old volcano slopes in East Africa and are dated at 20 Ma. This volcano slope forest habitat must have been very similar to that in which the mountain gorilla is found today.

The dryopithecine fossils range in time from 25 to 10 Ma. The African ones were earliest and the European and Asian fossils rather later. Had the world's climate not changed at this time the human evolutionary story might have been different; from 15 Ma to the close of the Miocene, 5 million years later, and then on into the **Pliocene**, a very slow but definite change in climatic conditions brought enormous changes in ecological adaptations in its wake. The great rain forests, deprived for some reason of a continuous and reliable precipitation, gave way to drier forests, with a deciduous leaf fall in the dry season. Plant forms would slowly have adapted to this change, the non-seasonal flowering and fruiting of trees characteristic of the rain forest must have given way to more fixed and seasonal patterns of fruit and seed dispersal. A more open type of woodland undoubtedly became widespread. We know from Miocene fossils that the small forest-living antelopes gave way to the larger grass-eating forms. Ruminants as we know them today were only just evolving. In this shift of climate the variety of fossil forms begins to increase greatly, presumably to fill a new diversity of habitats that had not existed before.

40

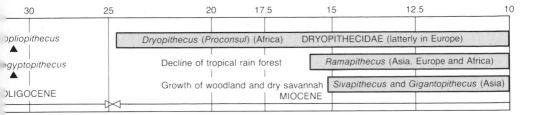

| 30 | 25 | 20 | 17.5 | 15 | 12.5 | 10 |

ppliopithecus ▲

gyptopithecus ▲

OLIGOCENE

Dryopithecus (Proconsul) (Africa)   DRYOPITHECIDAE (latterly in Europe)

Decline of tropical rain forest   *Ramapithecus* (Asia, Europe and Africa)

Growth of woodland and dry savannah   *Sivapithecus* and *Gigantopithecus* (Asia)

MIOCENE

6.3   *Ramapithecus*

Quite how the earliest human divergence from the older dryopithecines took place we cannot yet be sure, but it is clear that by 14 Ma new dietary feeding adaptations had evolved in more man-like apes suited to these drier environments. Man-like apes or hominids are peculiarly hard to define. The term **hominid** can be used to describe any fossil form that is on a broadly human ancestral line, which has departed from the lineage of the great apes and which shows features such as upright posture that are characteristically man-like rather than ape-like. The earliest clear hominids, such as *Australopithecus*, are only found in Africa, but some members of the extinct family of **Ramapithecidae** show definite early hominid connections. The best-known 'proto-hominids' from this family occur, not in Africa, but in the **Siwalik Hill** sediments at the foot of the Himalaya range in the Punjab province of Pakistan. Here the sediments span 13 million years of time and are a phenomenal 3000 metres in thickness. Such depths of sediment, formed by material carried off from the Himalayas, almost defy description. In the lowest levels of these sediments David Pilbeam's team have found, amongst thousands of fossils, over one hundred specimens of ramapithecine. *Ramapithecus*, from which the family takes its name, was first discovered in 1932 by Edward Lewis and named after the mythological Hindu deity Rama. This is one of the most important ramapithecines in any discussion of human origins. Although the specimens of *Ramapithecus* are very fragmented they have several special features. First, the canines are small and not large like those of the dryopithecines and pongids. This is a hominid feature. Secondly, the jaw is shorter and either more pointed at the front in a V-shape or has a more human **paraboloid** curved tooth row. Thirdly, the teeth are set in a deep jaw, are flattened and have enormously thickened enamel and larger biting surfaces than those of the pongids. So far fossils are too rudimentary to tell anything about locomotion in *Ramapithecus*. *Sivapithecus* is a similar form to *Ramapithecus* but with a larger body size and larger canines. *Gigantopithecus* as its name implies was an even more massive gorilla-sized genus in a similar mould. Both *Sivapithecus* and *Gigantopithecus* are unlikely to have been hominid ancestors but they conveniently group with *Ramapithecus* in one family. In Africa a possible ramapithecine ape very similar to the Asian *Ramapithecus* is known. This form, sometimes described as *Kenyapithecus*, is currently the object of further fossil searches.

How do we interpret these animals? First, the dental distinction is of

41

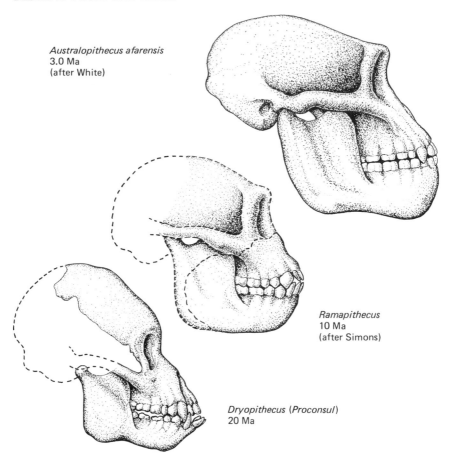

Australopithecus afarensis
3.0 Ma
(after White)

Ramapithecus
10 Ma
(after Simons)

Dryopithecus (Proconsul)
20 Ma

Figure 6.2   Early hominoids
Ramapithecus, for which few remains other than the face and jaws are known, was clearly better adapted for the sideways chewing of a harder vegetable diet than the earlier *Dryopithecus*. *Australopithecus* has the same reduced canines, more massive jaw and greatly thickened tooth enamel.

fundamental importance. It marks a break with the soft fruit- and leaf-eating style of the rain forest apes. Contemporary fossil species indicate an open woodland habitat for the ramapithecines. Their teeth are undoubtedly still herbivorous but adapted to a tougher drier vegetable diet. The thick tooth enamel could easily withstand the damage that might arise from eating hard seeds or small nuts in fruit. Thus it is envisaged that *Ramapithecus* was an opportunistic herbivore capable of feeding on a variety of dry whole fruits. Certainly, without protruding canines, sideways chewing would have been easier. Complete skeletal remains of *Ramapithecus* have not yet been found but this genus provides the best **proto-hominid** model to date. So far as the other Miocene apes are concerned, *Gigantopithecus* continued as a ground ape in Asia until a million years ago at least. Their massive molars turn up occasionally as "dragons teeth" in Chinese drug stores. *Sivapithecus* may well have evolved

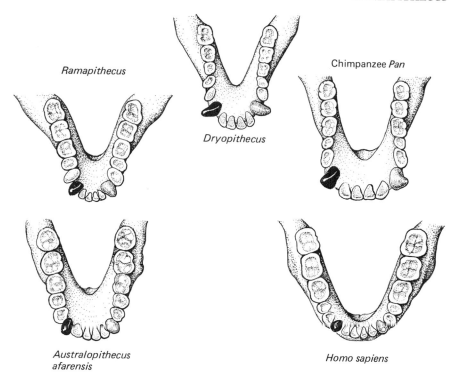

Figure 6.3   Jaw shapes and relative tooth sizes in hominoids (not to scale). *Dryopithecus* had only slightly 'V' shaped tooth rows. All of the modern apes have markedly 'U' shaped tooth rows, whilst *Ramapithecus* and early *Australopithecus* have more 'V' shaped tooth rows. In early and later man, the tooth row becomes more paraboloid. Note the relatively reduced canines of the *Ramapithecus* and two hominid jaws.

into the modern orangutan, for their facial and dental morphology is very similar. All other ramapithecines disappear from the fossil record by 9 Ma, and the ground-living cercopithecoid monkeys such as baboons become more common for the first time. The intriguing feature of the ramapithecine disappearance is that the earliest true hominids that appear in Ethiopia, Kenya and Tanzanian sites four million years later have the same thick enamelled teeth, low canines, V-shaped jaws and yet are upright bipedal walkers in open savannah. Thus the earliest australopithecines do show strong **phyletic** links with the ramapithecines, but the connection is **not** proven and more evidence will be needed for certainty.

An alternative view

This book follows the generally accepted view on hominid origins, the line of descent passing through a ramapithecine stage of harder toothed, dry woodland apes which possibly made the earliest bipedal adaptations. It has recently been suggested, on the basis of the 'molecular clock' used for comparing rates of change in animal proteins, that the chimpanzee and the gorilla diverged from the human line only in the last 4 to 5 million years and

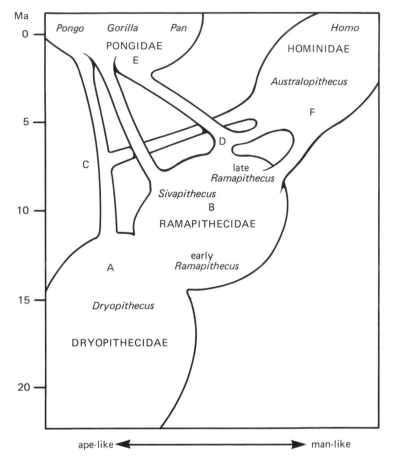

Figure 6.4 Possible evolutionary relationships between the principal hominoid families
The time axis (vertical) is set against a subjective ape-like to man-like axis. Hypothetical evolutionary pathways join the family clusters, in the absence of clear fossil evidence in between.
ABF Traditional view of hominid lineage
ACE Traditional view of pongid lineage
BE Probable orangutan lineage
ACE/ACF Possible route by-passing ramapithecid stage in the origin of African apes and man
ABDE Possible route to African apes if separation from hominids is very recent

not twelve to fifteen million years ago. This new view is cautiously approached by most palaeontologists from the basis of their own fossil evidence, for other estimates of the time that has passed since lineages have separated is essentially in accordance with much of the fossil record in those animal groups. Perhaps the chimpanzee evolved through a proto-hominid stage before becoming once again a forest-dwelling ape!

6.4 The evolution of bipedalism

What prompted the change from quadrupedalism to bipedalism? When did it occur? What advantages are there in bipedal walking and what disadvantages? Answers to these questions are really needed for a satisfactory understanding of this stage in human evolution.

Understanding the locomotor and skeletal adaptations of modern man

An evaluation of this evolutionary step requires a knowledge of the distinctive skeletal and locomotor features of man as a biped in contrast to quadrupeds. First, upright walking on two legs rather than on four involves a change in the position of the centre of gravity from above and between the four legs to above and between the two. In standing man, the centre of gravity is in the pelvic region and acts downwards just behind a line between the hip joints and in front of a line between the knee joints. As the femur is flexed forward in movement and the tibia flexed back, it will be clear that in standing upright on

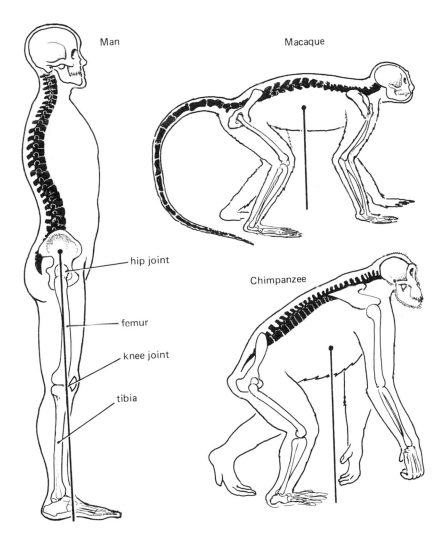

Figure 6.5 Bipedal and quadrupedal stances
In the quadrupedal macaque (*Cercopithecus*) the vertebral column is arched between pelvic and pectoral cantilever supports. In the more upright but still quadrupedal chimpanzee (*Pan*) the column is straighter. In man the vertebral column has reverse curvatures in the lumbar and cervical regions which bring the trunk and head above the centre of gravity.

45

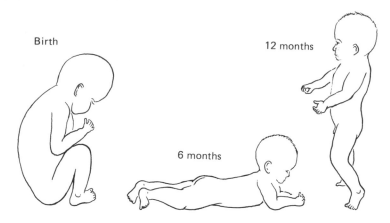

Birth

12 months

6 months

Figure 6.6   Growth changes to achieve bipedal posture
At birth the vertebral column is 'C' shaped. From two months onwards the neck retroflexion
develops whilst the lumbar secondary curvature develops when the infant learns to walk.

two legs, with the feet stabilised, a resting position is achieved whereby hip and
knee joints are locked in full extension. This position we know is restful and
requires little muscular tone for its maintenance. Again if the body is fully
upright and these two joints are fully flexed, there is a second restful position,
squatting, where again the centre of gravity acts downwards between the feet.
Both of these relaxed bipedal positions completely free the hands from helping
in the support of the body.

    In standing, the weight of the trunk and upper parts of the body is almost all
carried by the vertebral column acting down on the sacro-iliac. Quadrupedal
animals have an arched vertebral column from sacro-iliac to pectoral girdle,
cantilevered like a bridge by the downward forces of the rump and head.
Human infants are born with an arched **primary curvature** of the spine but
during infancy it undergoes **secondary curvature** by developing two **retroflexions** (bending the other way). The first retroflexion occurs in the baby's
neck, the cervical vertebrae curving backwards to raise the head up to face
forwards. The second, larger, retroflexion is in the small of the back where the
lumbar vertebrae centra and intervertebral discs expand more on the ventral
forward side, than they do dorsally, to become wedge-shaped cylindrical units.
This growth change occurs as the child learns to walk. The resulting sinuous
pillar of the spinal column has both compression strength and yet some
flexibility. Weight is transmitted, when standing, through the centra and
sacro-iliac to the pelvis, downwards through the femur head socket (ace-
tabulum), femur head and shaft to the knees. In man the knees are close
together beneath the centre of gravity, but the pelvis is broad to provide
adequate muscle attachment points for the striding gait. This has meant a
modification of the human femur. Compared to the apes, the femur has a
longer neck and the distal knee joint is angled to the shaft in order to articulate
horizontally. Despite this bringing in of the knees, under the centre of gravity,

when one leg is lifted as in walking there must be a tendency for the pelvis to drop down on the same side. This is countered in man by the contraction of **abductor muscles**, the **gluteus medius** and **gluteus minimus**, which run from the ilium (hip bone) to the top of the femur shaft. These abductor muscles contract on each side alternately and minimise pelvic tilting. The contraction occurs on the side on which you are standing in order to tilt laterally the pelvis and allow the swing through of the other leg. (See Fig. 6.7.)

In walking, the body leans forward and would fall were not the legs repeatedly, by forward flexion, brought beneath the trunk, then extended and pulled backwards in retraction to lift the body again. Once walking or running has begun, the body gains momentum and having achieved constant speed is carried almost upright. On decelerating it is thrown back from the hip and hence on coming to a stop again rests above the centre of gravity.

The human foot and ankle are also greatly modified. Compared to an ape's, the human ankle joint is fairly rigid and will not rotate easily left and right, but the foot can be pointed down well. There is a large **calcaneum** (heel bone) to which a well-developed Achilles tendon is attached, being the insertion of the soleus and gastrocnemius (calf muscles) and providing a means of powerfully extending the foot. If extension takes place during the stride, it will not be flat footed but will provide a propulsive and lifting force at each step. The whole structure of the human foot is modified for this extra propulsive element. Animals that walk on the flat of the foot rather than the toes are said to be **plantigrade**. The apes are plantigrade but they differ in having an unvaulted foot structure and an opposable toe (hallux). The human big toe is **not opposable** but aligned parallel with the others. The metatarsals are elongated and there is a **curved line of weight transmission** from the heel, through the outside edge of the foot to the ball of the foot and big toe. (Look at some wet foot prints on the floor.) There is also the **vaulted arch** from heel to ball on the inside. These modifications are considerable and must have taken many millions of years to perfect. In summary, the locomotor adaptation of modern man may be described as being a well-developed **bipedal plantigrade propulsive striding**.

The origins of upright walking

This background enables us to see the locomotor adaptations in modern man, but what evidence is there of intermediate developments? In the next chapter the extent of bipedalism in the earliest hominids is assessed, but we need to ask what advantages there were to any initial bipedalism. Quadrupedal apes did not just get up on their hind legs and walk out of the forest!

The first important question is whether the ramapithecines, or other protohominids, were quadrupedal. In that they were probably much more lightly built than chimpanzees, the suggestion has been made that they were **semi-brachiators**, much as young chimps are today. Dr E. A. Ashton of the Birmingham medical school has demonstrated, by multivariate analysis of different primate shoulder musculature systems, that the human shoulder is more mobile and better adapted for suspensory support than some shoulder systems of habitually quadrupedal primates such as baboons. The broad

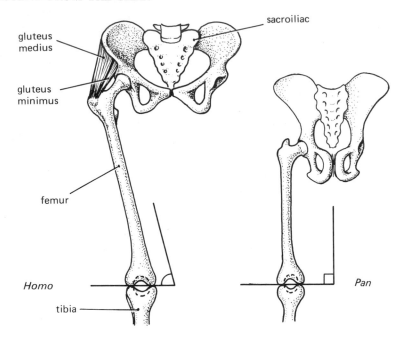

Figure 6.7   Human and chimpanzee femur and pelvic comparison
The gluteus muscles of the hip lifts the pelvis up so preventing tilting when the opposite leg is off the ground. Note that in man, unlike the ape, the knee joint is not at right angles to the femur shaft.

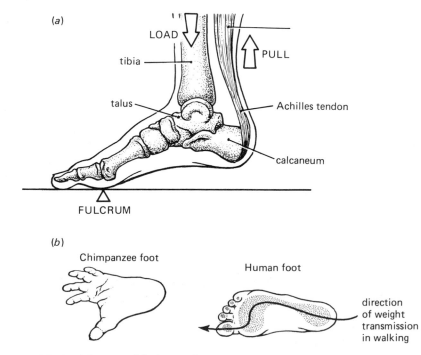

Figure 6.8   Modifications of the human foot

human chest and angled shoulders are good arm-swinging features. Observation of gibbons, which excel as brachiators, reveals that when on the ground they adopt a bipedal upright, but bowlegged, waddle, holding their hands free. If the protohominids came down to the ground already 'upright', as this gibbon model postulates, other advantages must have followed for bipedalism to become better established.

The disadvantages should be assessed first. Early bipedalism must have been a slow means of getting along; quadrupedal chimps and baboons today can outrun a man over a short distance at least. Vulnerability to new predators, now faced on the ground for the first time, may have been acute, for there were in the Pliocene primitive leopards and hyaenas from which safety could only be gained in the trees. Assuming a social troop structure, with many pairs of eyes, the safety aspect may not have been so severe a problem. So far as competition with other species went, there were no ground-living monkeys at that time.

The first advantage of bipedalism must undoubtedly have been the freedom of arms and hands to carry objects. Carrying and use of sticks, in defence, is known in chimpanzees, as is the collecting of bedding material for nest making. The carrying of infants is a well-developed primate character, but if the infant and mother were sedentary then male food-gathering and food-sharing may have been important. Erect, face-forward display may have been socially important within the troop as part of the sexual bonding between males and females, and upright displays giving the appearance of greater physical size may have been an advantage in facing predators. Savannah-dwelling monkeys today often stand upright to gain a better view. Certainly the height advantage might have been selected for early in bipedal evolution.

Once striding developed, selection forces would have operated in developing this new means of progression by increased length of stride, spring in the gait and changed pelvic shape and femoral angles. This must have been a slow process, but by 4.0 Ma the very earliest true hominid remains show that the apes had 'stood up'. By 3.6 Ma the **Laetoli footprints**, discovered by Mary Leakey's team, show an almost modern stride. This is one of the most remarkable fossil discoveries in recent years. A study of the footprint bed reveals that after a fresh volcanic carbonatite lava ash fall, an adult and two younger individuals walked across an open stretch of dry lake flats. Shortly after, rain turned this cement-like ash to solid rock for perpetuity. Analysis of the stride length indicates an adult height of about four or five feet. The smallest child's prints are right beside those of the adult and keeping step as if they were holding hands. The older child's steps follow behind those of the adult, each foot placed in the larger print impressions.

Figure 6.9   The Laetoli footprints
Three early hominids walked upright and left these footprints three and a half million years ago.
(M. D. Leakey, 1981)

7   The australopithecines: the man-apes of Africa

Our understanding of the australopithecines has been greatly influenced by the sequence and circumstances of their discovery and by the personalities and opinions that have prevailed since the 1920s. Almost all palaeoanthropologists agree that these **man–apes** first appeared more than four million years ago but only new finds from areas like Ethiopia will illuminate the problem of origins that Figure 6.3 illustrates. These early hominids were adapted to light woodland or savannah living and were, so far as we know, only found in the continent of Africa. They had an apparently herbivorous dentition, with relatively reduced canines and incisors if compared to modern apes but thicker enamel and larger crushing molars. They were almost fully bipedal but probably retained an acrobatic nimbleness in tree climbing in comparison with ourselves. They were small, only little more than a metre in height, but probably strong for their size. Whether they were in part ancestral to man is still debated, but it is certain that one species diverged increasingly from man in the direction of a more massive size and in consuming a bulk vegetable diet. What is not debated is that, of the diversity of forms which did evolve, all have now become extinct.

7.1   Discovery of the australopithecines

To some extent the early twentieth century notion of the 'missing link' prevented palaeontologists from recognising the australopithecines for what we now see them to be. At the time when Darwin's work was slowly becoming accepted the earliest discoveries of fossil man were such rudiments as the massive-browed skull of Neanderthal man, from Germany, and the equally large and heavy-browed skull cap of *Homo erectus* (originally called *Pithecanthropus*) from Java. Evolutionarily we now know that these are relatively recent forms, but to the contemporary view the word *Pithecanthropus*, 'ape man', implied a missing link that was a large-brained and intelligent creature before it adopted upright human form.

In 1912 the Piltdown forger (possibly William Sollas, Professor of Geology at Oxford University) played, no doubt unconsciously, on this image in his attempt to deceive professional rivals. Piltdown man was compounded of a human cranium and an orangutan jaw, the teeth filed down and colour stained to match the old brain case. It was a cleverly devised hoax for it was not revealed finally as a forgery until the advent of radio-carbon dating in the 1950s. With this 'ape man' notion in everybody's minds it was easy for contemporary palaeontologists to be dismissive of a small-brained ape fossil discovered in South Africa in 1924.

Raymond Dart obtained what is now called the **Taung baby** from a limestone quarry near Johannesburg, where he was then a young lecturer in

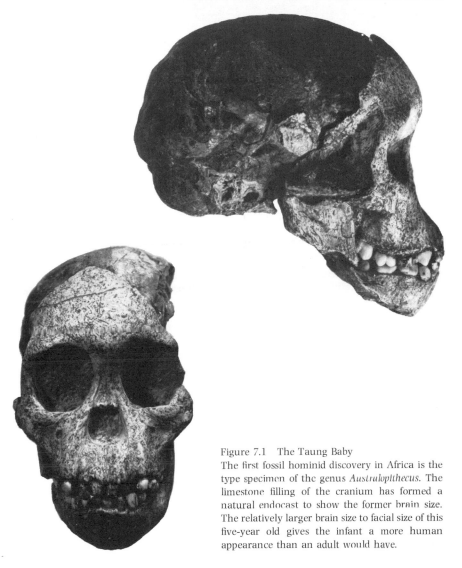

Figure 7.1 The Taung Baby
The first fossil hominid discovery in Africa is the type specimen of the genus *Australopithecus*. The limestone filling of the cranium has formed a natural endocast to show the former brain size. The relatively larger brain size to facial size of this five-year old gives the infant a more human appearance than an adult would have.

anatomy at the Witwatersrand University. It consisted of a limestone endocranial cast and a complete face and lower jaw. He recognised that its cranial volume, though small, was comparably larger than that of an ape, and that the teeth were of human type. Most importantly the **foramen magnum**, the hole at the back of the skull through which the spinal cord emerges, was below the brain case and not positioned further back as in the apes. With some excitement he published an account of his upright 'southern ape' and named it *Australopithecus africanus* suggesting a position for it intermediate between apes and man. After Piltdown man's discovery, prevailing opinion in Britain was hostile to this interpretation and what support Dart had from Britain was from William Sollas, perhaps the one man who knew that Piltdown was a hoax.

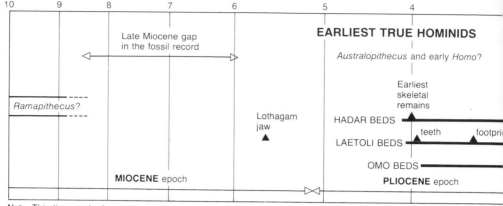

Late Miocene gap
in the fossil record

EARLIEST TRUE HOMINIDS

Australopithecus and early *Homo*?

Earliest
skeletal
remains

Ramapithecus?

Lothagam
jaw

HADAR BEDS

teeth   footpri

LAETOLI BEDS

OMO BEDS

MIOCENE epoch

PLIOCENE epoch

Note: This time scale does not attempt to group the hominid fossils phylogenetically.
For possible relationships see Figure 7.4.

Australopithecus thus had a poorly heralded start. But a colleague of Dart's, **Robert Broom**, a well-known South African palaeontologist, took up Dart's interest and became convinced that other early men might be found in the continent. Twelve years later he made his first discovery of a larger-skulled adult australopithecine at **Sterkfontein**. This site, like two more he discovered at **Kromdraai** and **Swartkrans**, were vertical fissure limestone caves that had been filled in from the top. The fossils were well preserved though almost concretely fast in rock. To his surprise, the second two caves bore remains that were remarkably different, for here the skulls and teeth of the man-like apes were more massive and certainly more primitive looking. Broom gave a whole constellation of names to these new finds; the **robust** heavily-built forms he placed in the genus *Paranthropus* and the more slender, lightly-built **gracile** forms in the genus *Plesianthropus*. Dart, although an anatomist by profession, returned to fossil hunting in 1947 at a fifth limestone cave site at **Makapansgat**. Here he unearthed very large numbers of fragmentary australopithecine fossils, largely the crushed remains of what were clearly leopard prey and hyaena scavengings. Dart attributed, we now believe mistakenly, carnivorous and cannibal tendencies to his little apes. He even thought that those at Makapansgat had domesticated fire. He thus added *Australopithecus prometheus* to the list of fossil species. There were now three genera and a further was soon to follow.

By the late 1950s few doubted that Africa sustained more hope of yielding good fossils of early man than anywhere else. Further north from South Africa, in Kenya, a distinguished archaeologist and Kikuyu linguist called **Louis Leakey** was increasingly turning his attention to fossil hunting. The son of English missionaries, he knew East Africa well. He had already made considerable advances in the knowledge of African prehistory, but a deep series of sediments at **Olduvai** in northern Tanzania had attracted his particular interest for it was extraordinarily rich in fossils. We now know, by the new dating techniques, that the lowest beds, revealed by the cutting of a river gorge, are between 1.5 and 1.9 million years old. Here Louis and his wife Mary Leakey made the discovery in 1959 of the most perfect australopithecine skull yet found. Seized by that feeling of uniqueness and pride in one's discovery that

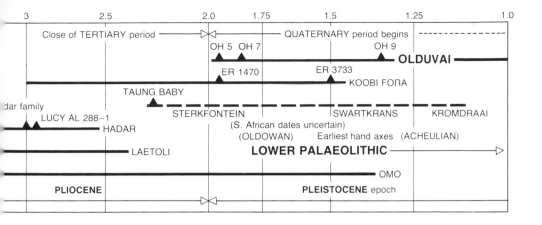

is the palaeontologist's chief reward, they named the fossil by yet a further new name, *Zinjanthropus boisei*, **nutcracker man** (OH5) for the molars of this fossil were prodigious. Louis Leakey's considerable knowledge of archaeology came in at this point for he had also found very primitive stone tools in the Olduvai beds and he soon became convinced that these were the work of early man and not this massive-jawed man–ape. Extensive progress has been made by Louis Leakey (who died in 1975), his wife Mary and the teams of collaborators working at this site in the years following this early discovery. Olduvai is perhaps the best documented fossil site anywhere in the world. The Leakeys' son Richard has worked fossil sites further to the north at **Koobi Fora** on the shores of **Lake Turkana** (formerly called Lake Rudolph) and in the great **Omo** river region that drains south into that lake from the Ethiopian highlands. Koobi Fora sediments span a period of time back to 3.0 Ma and a diversity of human and australopithecine forms are revealed. International teams in recent years have produced many more remains of hominids showing clearly that at least two, and probably more, different forms co-existed. Even earlier sediments which overlap Koobi Fora and Omo in time, are found at **Laetoli**, in Tanzania, and at **Hadar**, in Ethiopia. Here the most recent significant collections have been made and the most ancient australopithecines discovered. Mary Leakey has worked the Laetoli site and Don Johanson and team those in Ethiopia. From this abundance of new evidence an intelligible pattern is emerging, but the picture is complex and easy answers cannot be given. Two excellent books, by Don Johanson and Richard Leakey respectively, cover this recent period. Patient study is needed if the evidence as a whole is to be understood.

7.2 *Australopithecus* species

The semantic difference between an **ape-man** and a **man-ape** is not worth arguing, but the term ape-man raises in the mind science fiction and cinematic images that are likely to mislead. To describe australopithecines therefore as man-apes perhaps only dodges the stereotype but it does add emphasis to the word ape, for they were apes with human characteristics and not brutish and hairy men.

Australopithecus afarensis

The early hominid story is in limbo between four and eight million years ago. Don Johanson refers to this fossil gap as a 'black-hole' for no light has yet come out of it to illumine the problem of either an immediate African ape ancestry for man, or a clear ramapithecine affinity. The extremely fragmentary fossils that exist are of a small unspecialised ape-like form comparable *in size* to a chimpanzee. This ape affinity is very marked in the earliest good fossils from Hadar, unearthed by the Berkeley California team led by Don Johanson, and is typified by the fossil **Lucy** (AL 288–1). Discovered in 1974, this almost complete fossil individual was immediately seen to be a hominid for the pelvis was of a characteristically human form and from the width of its birth canal demonstrably female. Lucy obtained her name from the Beatles' pop-song, 'Lucy in the sky with diamonds', as this was being played in camp on the night of her fortuitous discovery. Other specimens of more fragmented individuals of mixed ages from site 333, who may have been drowned together in a gully flash flood, are of the same species. There also seems little doubt now that more fragmentary tooth and jaw remains from **Lothagam** and Laetoli belong to the one species. In view of the full bipedal adaptation of Lucy's pelvis and femur head, there seems no reason to doubt that this species was responsible for the exactly contemporary Laetoli footprints. So close are these fossil specimens to a single general type that Johanson and many others ascribe this earliest form to the species *Australopithecus afarensis*, named after the **Afar** region of Ethiopia. The fossils of this earliest form, dating from 4.0 Ma, are now as well known as the later australopithecines and from their novelty do indeed justify a new name.

Contemporary bedded fossils indicate that these earliest australopithecines were woodland or treed-savannah dwellers. They varied in height, as adults, from 1–1.5 metres, but they were thick-boned and of muscular build, being from 30–70 kg in weight. Thus, although only of the stature of present-day primary school children, they would have been formidably tough and agile. From the femur shape there is no doubt that they walked bipedally, but the pelvis is not fully of human form nor indeed are the foot bones of the later australopithecines that are better known. E. H. Ashton of Birmingham University is sure that their gait was more rolling than our own, the stabilising power of the lesser gluteal muscles being underdeveloped. The Laetoli footprints show an already arched foot suggesting some propulsive foot extension. Given the greater arm length to leg length ratio, than in modern man, obvious hip and shoulder mobility and evidence of considerable ape-like wrist bones and more curled fingers, one must conclude that they were also still very at home in the trees. Modern human adults only have to look at the tree-climbing ease and acrobatic skill of small children to realise that they have literally grown out of the arboreal habit. Early australopithecines should be viewed as creatures for which trees were probably important, as a refuge from predators as well as sources of picked plant food.

The image of a very human albeit diminutive body is clear, but the skulls are remarkably ape-like in this early form. The range of cranial volumes, which is equivalent to brain size, is 380–450 cm³; that for chimpanzees is 300–400 cm³.

Figure 7.2   A reconstruction of *Australopithecus afarensis* (based upon the work of Jay Matternes)

This is certainly nowhere near the 1 345 cm³ mean for modern man (see Appendix II). Their jaws were relatively large, however, but showing the adaptations foreshadowed in the ramapithecines of thick, enamelled, flattened teeth adapted for extensive chewing of food. There is evidence that canine reduction from ape-like form was recent, for in some jaws, probably those of males, the canines are modest, somewhat pointed and protruding from the tooth row but worn flat at the tips. The more V-shaped jaw, such as Lucy's, may well be from females with smaller front teeth. To our human view of a face, they were **prognathous**, with forward-jutting jaws and lips, in marked contrast to their low-crowned heads, flattened faces with little nose and no chin protruding below. Figure 7.2 is based upon a reconstruction of the facial features of *Australopithecus afarensis* by the anatomical artist Jay Matternes.

This very ape-headed australopithecine *A. afarensis*, is absent from the top horizons at Hadar at around 2.8 Ma. Either before or just after this time what looks like speciation, of the cladogenic kind, took place from the primitive hominid stock. It is now clear that by 2.3 Ma there were some larger brained but still big toothed hominids which by 2.0 ma were active tool makers. Such undoubted human ancestors must be placed in the genus *Homo*. These earliest true men are described in the next chapter, but what is quite clear is that other hominids, australopithecines, were contemporary with them. These later man-apes are broadly divisible into gracile and robust forms.

Australopithecus africanus

Australopithecus africanus, represented originally by the Taung baby, is the least easily defined of all the australopithecines, largely because of its intermediate position: intermediate in time and in possible phyletic branchings of the hominid stock. It was a lightly built, **gracile**, form in comparison with the later robust ones. It thus fits well onto a line of phyletic descent from *Australopithecus afarensis* and clearly follows on well as an antecedent of the robust species. Thus specimens that are still relatively small-brained and not massively-molar toothed are ascribed to this species. All of the *A. africanus* specimens can be dated between 2.7 and 2.2 million years. Broom's Sterkfontein *Plesianthropus* is now considered to be of this species.

Ecologically this was again an open woodland or savannah dweller. They differed from the early australopithecines in being of generally larger size and were noticeably bigger brained, but still very heavy jawed. Cranial capacities range from 375–575 cm^3 with a mean of 450 cm^3. There is a great range in size of bone specimens and again a hint of size difference between sexes. We know little of their way of life. It is perhaps best to regard them as very generalised rather than specialised, perhaps a polytypic species, with many variant forms, with versatility in diet and habitat. There is no firm association between this species and early stone tools and supposition alone that any hunting or scavenged-meat eating was adopted. The gathering and sharing of food may have become more widespread amongst hominids at this stage of evolution but that too is impossible to prove. Certainly most anthropologists now feel that the notions propagated by Robert Ardrey in books, such as *African Genesis*, of blood-thirsty, club-carrying ape-men, who bludgeoned baboons and each other to death, are mistaken.

Australopithecus robustus/boisei

The **robust** australopithecines, represented first by the *Paranthropus* specimens of Broom from South Africa, have long been problematic but now clearly appear to be a side issue so far as human evolution is concerned. Absolute dating of the Swartkrans remains is impossible because of the lack of volcanic rock for potassium–argon dating, but what is significant is that the fauna associated with these fossils is more modern whilst that at the other *A. africanus* sites in South Africa is clearly older, many of the animal forms being extinct. Broom was convinced of the greater 'primitiveness' or antiquity of the robust forms but it seems that they may in fact be younger, that is more recent;

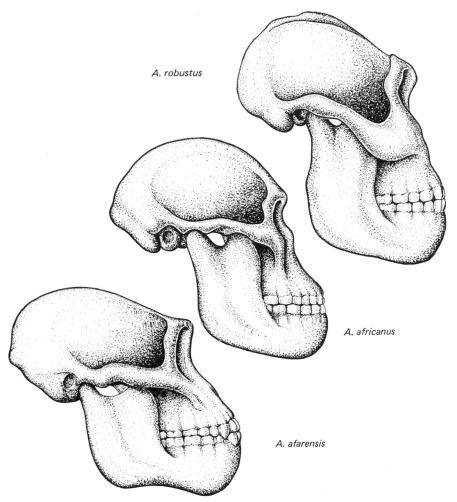

A. robustus

A. africanus

A. afarensis

Figure 7.3   The Australopithecines
The three species of *Australopithecus* may be separated either in time or to some extent be contemporary. The largest, *Australopithecus robustus*, is the most specialised of the man-apes being adapted for the mighty chewing of a vegetable diet.

robustness followed gracility. All of the East African robust forms are often referred to as the species *A. boisei*, using Louis Leakey's original *Zinjanthropus boisei* epithet, and are radiometrically dated between about 2 and 1 million years ago. *A. boisei* is either regarded as a different geographical race or separate species. We are thus obliged to see these massive-molared man-apes as a later offshoot of the early australopithecines which became extinct within the last million years in Africa. In this respect they parallel the *Gigantopithecus* ground ape of Asia, perhaps the best candidate for any truth in the yeti myth.

The distinctive features of the robust australopithecines are their overall greater size and the extensive modification of skull and jaw features for mighty chewing. At Harvard, Alan Walker, an English colleague of Richard Leakey, has studied the robust australopithecine teeth and jaws. In the largest forms the incisors and canines are much reduced and the molars greatly enlarged and flattened. The jaw is deep and strongly buttressed with bone, whilst the rather flat cranium has a median **sagittal** crest of bone, as in the gorilla, to which massive **temporalis** muscles, used in the chewing mechanism, would have attached. These features all suggest that this larger australopithecine, standing all of 5 foot high (1.8 metres) and weighing quite as much as a modern man, spent much of its time chewing a hard vegetable diet. Walker's study of the enamel thickness and surface microwear show no scratches that could be associated with a diet containing soil particles or bone. This seems to rule out meat, root and even herb-leaf eating. The thick enamel would have protected the tooth from cracking if very small hard seeds were present. Walker therefore sees the robusts as predominantly eaters of fruit, both soft- and hard-cased, possibly in less open but more wooded environments. Certainly if this low-energy and low-protein vegetarian diet was to sustain such a large non-ruminant such bulk eating is a solution.

Sexual dimorphism, the difference in size and proportion between males and females, was once seriously proposed as an explanation of the robust (male) and gracile (female) forms. Given our current knowledge of fossil dating, it is far-fetched to ascribe these form differences to sex alone, but within the diversity of fossils at any one time we should expect there to be some genetical, sex-governed, size and proportion differences. Certainly Koobi Fora robust

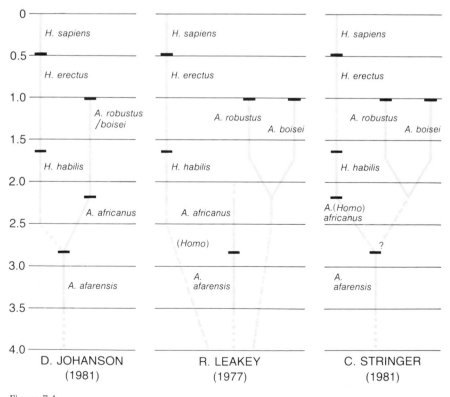

Figure 7.4

australopithecines are found in two size classes, larger males and smaller females.

The brain size of the robust species is in the range 410–600 cm³ with a mean of 504 cm³. For their size they were not necessarily more intelligent than the other australopithecines, indeed such a brain volume is comparable to that of the gorilla. Size and scaling considerations provide one of the best reasons for thinking that these latter-day man-apes were merely larger versions of the earlier australopithecines. Such **allometry** (change in proportion with growth change in size) cannot however explain the sudden brain volume increases that occurred in the rise of the genus *Homo* (see Appendix II).

7.3 Australopithecines and human origins

Richard Leakey and other palaeontologists see the diversity of species, sexual dimorphism of species and ecological niche diversity as more complex than is presented here. Others take a minimalist route, not postulating more than the most direct pathway. Students of this subject must therefore adopt an open, but not simplistic, view. Figure 7.4 presents three views of early hominid phylogeny, all recently postulated. The differences between the diagrams are not so much ones of delineating the span of phyletic species but of determining when cladogenic species diversification occurred and which species gave rise to which. R. Leakey prefers to keep the australopithecines at a distance from *Homo*. Johanson, with a possibly over-inflated view of the significance of *A. afarensis*, considers this species the hominid prototype. Stringer, of the British Museum of Natural History, inclines to the view that *A. africanus* was most probably ancestral to *Homo*. What is in no doubt is that speciation at some point occurred and that one line led to man.

8 *Homo habilis:* the making of mankind

Homo habilis crosses the threshold from man-apes to man. Besides fulfilling the traditional archaeological criterion for inclusion in the genus *Homo*, **the making of tools**, this species clearly demonstrates the expansion of brain size that presages the development of those characteristically human social attributes, intellectual and linguistic powers and fine manipulative skills. This process of becoming human in a biological and social sense is often called **hominisation**. It will have become clear to the reader that other primates hint at human nature, but there was a threshold point in evolution, reached two or three million years ago, when development towards humankind had an autocatalytic effect that furthered the hominisation process. This chapter is concerned with these largely hypothetical developments and to a lesser extent the *Homo habilis* remains that support the ideas. Fossils can only tell so much but we are able by careful reasoning and logical deduction to suggest how the gaps in our evidence may be filled.

A mosaic of influences is now believed to contribute to hominisation. Principally important are **food sharing**, the development of **manipulative skills**, the development of **speech and language**, an **extended period of childhood** for learning, a change in sexuality to allow **pair bonding** and interwoven through all of these the **expansion and sophistication of the brain**.

8.1 Food sharing

Food sharing is a characteristically human activity. Sitting down to a meal together is a central feature of everyone's culture. Feeding behaviour in all living primate species is unlike this, for food is selected and consumed by individuals in their social group as they range in search of it. There is, of course, in such animals some assisted feeding of weaning infants and some token exchange of food by adults, but purposive gathering of food and return to a home base for shared consumption is human alone. There is now good archaeological evidence that late *Homo habilis* butchered carcases and shared food at a home base. If the earliest hominids had infants with long periods of childhood, a home base, even if only temporary, was essential. A **division of labour** may also have begun, with males operating in bands together at a greater radius from the home base than the females. In ranging out to gather and scavenge for food what these now bipedal hominids were able to carry home in their freed hands may have taken on a special social significance. The **food sharing hypothesis** is often regarded today as the starting point of human cultural evolution.

8.2 Hands

Hands, the characteristically modified forelimbs of primates, differ from paws

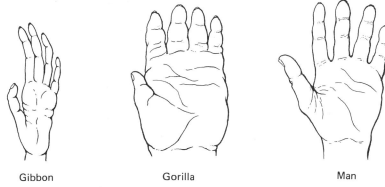

| Gibbon | Gorilla | Man |

Figure 8.1   The hands of primates

in having **prehensility**, that ability to pick up objects between thumb base and finger tips, and **opposability**, whereby the thumb can grip against the other digits and hold on to an object. The degree to which the hands of primates are strongly prehensile or finely opposable varies greatly, but in man alone is the hand most fully modified and most dextrously controlled. The most significant anatomical adaptation, distinguishing the hand of man from ape, is first a highly mobile basal thumb joint, the basal phalange of the pollex, or thumb, having a saddle-shaped rocking articulation. Secondly, the terminal thumb bone, bearing the nail, is relatively elongated and broadened to support the pad at the end of the digit. Apes have hands that are largely adapted for locomotion rather than for fine manipulation. For example, the gibbon has a very small thumb that does not interfere with the brachiating hooking grasp of their elongated fingers. The gorilla has a much curled hand with solid foot-sole like knuckles. The great apes are seemingly clumsy by our standards of dexterity and although skilled by animal standards give the impression that great concentration and effort are needed to manipulate any fine object.

Man has two types of grip, a prehensile **power grip** for actions requiring the application of strength and a **precision grip** in which the thumb pad opposes the tips of the other digits. Thus we use a power grip to a tennis racket and a precision grip to a pen. Man's finely controlled individual finger and hand movements are a product of very considerable motor cortical development in the association areas of the brain.

The species name *habilis*, meaning 'handy' or 'dextrous', was given by Louis Leakey in 1964 to the hominid remains associated with the earliest tools at Olduvai. The fingers of *Homo habilis* were slightly incurved, the thumb was only a little shorter than ours with a shorter terminal phalanx. With its small brain, nervous control may have limited the hand's usefulness somewhat, but the earliest stone tools could have been made without difficulty using a power grip alone. The relationship between hand and brain lies behind the evolution of the most primitive technologies. Although earlier hominids were undoubtedly tool users, perhaps using sticks as chimpanzees do, and may have modified them for use, man was the first purposive maker of tool kits of selected and worked implements. *Homo habilis*, 'handy man' launched the first stone-tool culture, the **Lower Palaeolithic** (see Chapter 9).

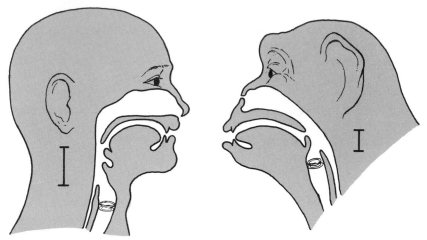

Figure 8.2   The ape and human vocal apparatus
Compared to the ape, man has a much larger vocal chamber with a greater capacity for voice modification. It is believed that apes are unable to communicate by speech sounds, not because of this deficiency alone but because of a lack of brain control for the throat muscles involved in sound production.

8.3   Speech and language

Apes do not talk, but some people never seem to cease from this peculiarly human activity. Speech and cultural transmission through language are human characteristics and although apes may grimace, gesticulate and hoot to communicate with each other, they have no syntactic language in which symbols with meaning are consecutively ordered to convey sustained transmissions of information.

Anatomically the apes have a very short pharynx, between the buccal cavity and vocal cords of the larynx, the palate is flattened and the tongue shallow rooted. In man, perhaps due in part to his upright stance and retracted face, the pharynx is deep, the palate arched and the tongue deep rooted to form the anterior wall of the vocal chamber. With better tongue and lip control and this muscular throat chamber, man has a greater capacity for vocal modification in the production of sound. Clearly such anatomical differences alone cannot account for the apes' incapacity to learn vocal speech control, even when reared for years in the company of human teachers. The ape may ape but he cannot parrot!

In order to puzzle this out, many studies have recently been done on both ape language-learning and intelligence. First, chimpanzees are undoubtedly very intelligent animals, using their ample abilities for learning to cope with complex social situations and no doubt also, in the wild, to find and remember the numerous geographical localities of their home range. Socially they are sophisticated and as individuals manifest a degree of awareness of themselves that better enables them to interact with other individuals. They are 'self' conscious, for they undoubtedly do recognise themselves as themselves in a mirror, something that other mammals apparently do not. Of the many attempts that have been made to teach apes language, only those involving

signing with the fingers or utilising visual object symbols have had much success. American Sign Language (ASL), used by the deaf and dumb, has particular signed words. Thus visual symbols, or even words represented by differently coloured plastic tokens, may be taught to give a chimp a vocabulary of over one hundred word symbols. Such, now famous, apes as Washoe, Sarah and Nim have learned thereby to communicate wants, but they show little evidence of the mental processes required to build linked sequences of symbols to convey varied meaning. They have no syntax, no ordered grammar. Thus Washoe, an experienced ASL signer, desperately wanting a drink of orange squash from his trainer would sign 'drink-sweet-please-hurry' or 'sweet-hurry-drink-please' or 'hurry-drink-sweet-please' without apparent attention to word sequence. Only after six years of training was Sarah, whose language consisted of plastic-tokens, able to follow a short sequence of instructions with 80% success. It thus seems that apes can only be trained to the linguistic capacity of two-year-old human infants. This is not just deficient control of lips, tongue and larynx but the chimp brain's inability to associate such vocal control with meaning and a further inability to sequence word symbols grammatically.

Two areas of the human brain apparently work together to make human speech and language possible. They are named after two neuroanatomists and are called Broca's and Wernicke's areas. **Broca's area** in the left frontal lobe is

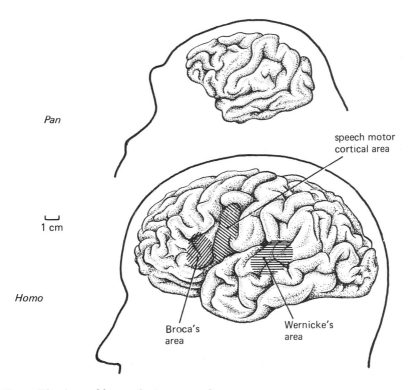

Figure 8.3 Ape and human brain compared

concerned with grammatical word form and sequence, that is syntax, and acts as the coordinating centre that instructs the motor cortical areas, just posterior to it, controlling the lips, tongue and larynx. **Wernicke's area** is in the left temporal lobe and is the major centre for storage of auditory, visual and verbal (hence also heard and read) memory. Wernicke's area is thus the word bank and Broca's area the synthesiser acting under the higher centres of the brain. It should be noted that this activity is localised in the left hemisphere almost exclusively. Such lateralised specialisation is a brain feature of man. Neurological investigation of chimpanzee brains reveals that both of these areas are very rudimentary and undeveloped in complexity.

Traces of the early evolutionary development of these specialised brain areas are intriguingly revealed on the inner surfaces of fossil crania, for during life the outer brain membranes and blood vessels, that closely follow the brain's convoluted contours, become imprinted in the surrounding cranial bone. **Endocasts** of hominid crania have been minutely studied by Ralph Holloway, of Columbia University, who has shown most convincingly that the left hemisphere **frontal**, **parietal** and **temporal** lobes of *A. africanus* and *H. habilis* already have speech centre developments to a markedly greater extent than the modern apes. Thus the anatomical linguistic centres seem to have specialised ahead of general brain expansion. This is the only real clue we have that early hominids may have begun not just speech but also the exchange of ideas and information. Noisy vocalisation may have been an important adaptation for the very earliest hominids, particularly in defensive threat displays against carnivores. Such a pre-adaptation, to hoot *specific* signal warnings, may have been the neurological basis for these later more complex speech developments.

8.4   Extended childhood

Any student still at school or college might regard this human characteristic rather cynically, but an extended childhood with prolonged learning opportunities before the adult world is faced has been the strategy that alone has allowed man to cope with life in such a complex world.

Early in primate evolution a reproductive strategy evolved in which single young were carried by their mother in an arboreal environment. This early selective pressure favoured a greater investment in the foetus of maternal energy and nutrients, enabling a larger-brained child to be born. Brain cells are peculiar in very largely completing their tissue development in foetal life. Brainy infants may therefore become brainy adults, but only if the infant brain with its increased storage capacity develops by the process of learning, for in all higher mammals the innate, inborn abilities are few and the learned ones paramount.

A single infant in a social species is born into a favourable environment for learning. **Play**, an activity embracing in essence all the adult activities of feeding, fighting and social and sexual interaction, equips the young individual for society. The more fully prepared the young are the stronger the society will be. Once the childhood period is extended, however, children remain children for longer and mothers cannot easily care for more than one

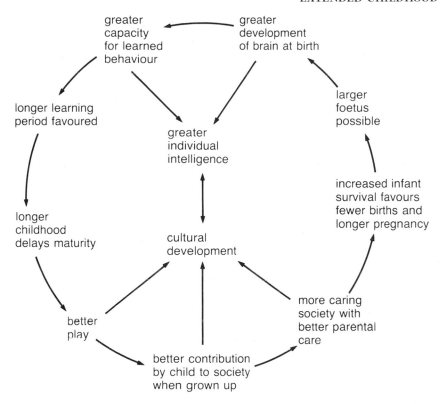

Figure 8.4 A positive feedback cycle showing the importance of extended childhood in the intellectual and cultural development of man

at a time. But offspring that are weaned may continue learning and growing whilst away from mother within the wider adoptive social group. Here arboreal life limits the process for it is harder for the vulnerable young to be kept together. For the earliest hominids this would undoubtedly have been easier with a ground-level home base served by a food-sharing society. Only in the most social and caring milieu is the childhood extension thus practicable, but it then becomes self-fuelling for the well-cared-for individual generates the more caring society. As effective social support of the young increases so their improved rate of survival reduces the species' requirement for any rapid reproductive rate. Maternal investment in the foetus, before birth, and in the nursed infants, after birth, may thereby be increased. Figure 8.4 summarises this positive feedback relationship. As has earlier been noted the *A. afarensis* female, Lucy, had no pelvic modification for a large-brained infant and Lucy herself had a chimp-sized brain. The same is not true of *A. africanus* pelves or those of early *Homo*, where the birth canal is of markedly extended size in the female and clearly adapted to giving birth to the larger-headed baby. It is also notable that the human infant, just before birth, has soft, only partially ossified, plates around the brain and is thereby adapted to squeezing through the pelvic aperture to start life with this greater brain-tissue complexity.

8.5 Changed sexuality

Female apes have a monthly cycle in which sexual receptiveness to mating by males only occurs around the time of ovulation. The chimpanzee female, for example, exhibits swollen genitalia and reddened skin around the vaginal opening for two to five days. During this **oestrous** period, by her scent and colouration, she attracts the promiscuous males and although weak honeymoon bondings occur with single male individuals for a few days, such liaison is generally all over after a week and any sexual approaches by males will be resisted. If the female has not become pregnant an oestrous period develops again some 30 days later. That early hominids had menstrual cycles of a human kind is unlikely for the human female cycle is physiologically unique amongst primates. There is no 'heat' or oestrous period, only a monthly renewal of the endometrium of the uterus. Secondly, in all 'primitive' human societies man and wife **pair-bonding** in marriage is the general rule, polygamy and promiscuity the exception. What caused this sexual transformation?

Perhaps the most plausible view of the evolution of enduring pair-bonding relates to the settled home base and the sexual division of labour envisaged in the food-sharing hypothesis. Social harmony is not favoured if there is a division of labour between males and females, such that they are segregated by day, whilst single females within the group become so attractive and only for one short time. The males, as in a troop of chimpanzees or baboons, would just not go away to gather food if individual females were 'on heat'. If on the other hand the receptive period of any one female is lengthened and the sexual signals of receptivity are reduced the problem is eased. If at the same time the selection of consorts is based on a broader mate preference than sex drives alone the social system might evolve in favour of more long-lasting sexual liaisons. We can envisage males soliciting females with gathered gifts and females soliciting males with more permanent sexual signals. This then might make that crucial bond, cemented by sexual activity, the survival advantage of which is the extended care of the bonded couple to their offspring. Families, however, are not self-sufficient and such a stabilised society of more or less bonded individuals would have greater survival advantage under natural selection if their family altruism extended to the whole group.

8.6 Brains and better brains

Hominisation is thus highly complex, a weaving together of food sharing, division of labour, new manual skills, speech and culture, prolonged childhood and the development of pair-bonded families and cohesive bands. It cannot all have happened at once, but imperceptibly slowly. Judging from our knowledge of other primates much of this hominisation may predate the origins of the genus *Homo*. But there is, however, a positive feedback, self-fuelling drive to the processes described in this chapter. It is not just a question of bigger brains but better ones. The brain became larger in volume but also increased the outer brain **cortical tissue** area, the grey matter, concerned with brain control. In the chimpanzee 25% of the surface grey matter is infolded but in *H. sapiens* 65% is infolded to give an increased neurological control much greater than the volume change, from 400 to 1 400 cm^3, implies. Particular brain areas

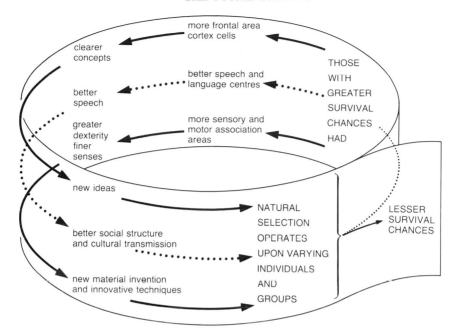

Figure 8.5   A theoretical scheme of positive feedback favouring the evolution of a more complex brain

have also developed far greater size and complexity, particularly the **frontal**, **parietal** and **temporal lobes**. Figure 8.5 attempts to show how natural selection acting upon individuals and groups, with necessarily genetically varied degrees of brain complexity, leads, by survival of the fittest, to further expansion and greater intricacy of function.

8.7   The fossil evidence for *Homo habilis*

The fossil evidence of early members of the genus *Homo* is scanty and not as well defined as would be desirable. Increased brain size above *A. africanus* levels, modern hand bones, enlarged pelves and no great increase in cheek teeth molarisation or decrease in incisor size, and consequently less massive jaws, are the diagnostic features that distinguish them from the australopithecines. The more robust the latter became the easier the distinction between the fossils becomes.

   Homo habilis evidence spans a period of time from just over two million to about 1.5 Ma. So far fossils of this species only come from Eastern Africa, whereas the sequel species *Homo erectus* is found throughout the Old World of Europe, Asia and Africa. The **H. habilis type specimen** (OH.7), described in 1969, comes from the lowest Bed I of the Olduvai Series. This consists of a very human jaw, albeit narrowed and fine, and some fragments of the parietal bones indicating a brain volume of 650 cm³. Hand bones, probably of the same individual, are virtually modern though differing as described earlier in this chapter. The best fossil skull is from Koobi Fora, not Olduvai, the celebrated **ER 1470** found by Bernard Ngeneo and carefully reconstructed by Richard Leakey's team in 1972. This fossil is dated at about 2 Ma, although initially

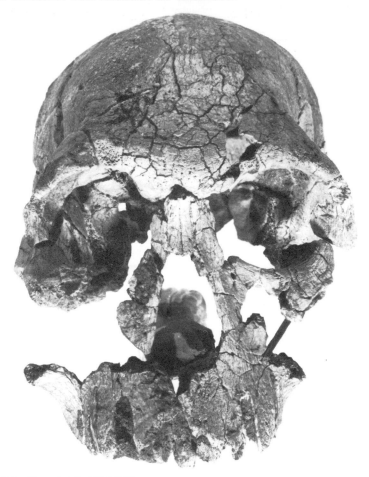

Figure 8.6   *Homo habilis* (ER 1470)
Dating from almost two million years ago, ER 1470 is one of the earliest definitively human remains.

thought to be older. ER 1470 was eroded out of sandy sediments as a large number of fractured pieces, but recombines in restoration to form an almost complete upper jaw, face and cranium. The cranial volume of 800 cm^3 is over 1.5 times that which would be expected in a comparably-sized ape. The rest of the facial features are similar to those of the australopithecines but the jaw was less massive though equally prognathous. With the lighter jaw and larger brain *Homo habilis* would have been more recognisably human than the portrait of Lucy, and certainly in stature the species was much closer to modern man.

This chapter on hominisation and evidence for *Homo habilis* has given extensive cover to the **hypothesis-making** that needs to be part of the scientific investigation if steps in evolution are to be proven to have occurred. It is very subjective, but if the hypothesis is plausible and simple and the fossils fit the hypothesis the plausibility increases. Such is the nature of our 'certainty' about these events.

9 *Homo erectus*: stone tools, hunting and fire

Eugene Dubois, a young Dutchman, stimulated by the implications for man's ancestory implicit in Darwin's theory, determined at an early age to find the missing link. He decided logically to look in a forested region of the tropics where apes were still found wild and where glaciations, as in Europe, had not eroded away the deep sediments in which these remains might be found. Unable to afford the cost of mounting his own expedition to **Java**, he joined the Dutch colonial army and in 1891, having been given charge of a group of prisoners who he turned to fossil excavating, he found what he had always longed to find, his ape-man, *Pithecanthropus*. The few teeth, skull cap and femur bone from the banked sediments of the Solo river, at a place called **Trinil**, constitute the type specimen of *Pithecanthropus erectus*. The skull was so thick and low brow ridged that ape affinities were suspected, but the brain volume, 850 cm³, was relatively large and the femur was of an upright, erect, hominid. Here was the ape-man that popular image sought and as such it was announced to the world by a jubilant Dubois. In the early part of this century increasing numbers of fossils of early man revealed the same general features as Dubois' fossil. These are now therefore lumped together in the genus *Homo*, the name *Pithecanthropus* becoming obsolete, although the specific name *erectus* remains. The characteristically thick, low-domed skulls of *Homo erectus* are found from Africa, Europe and Asia between 1.6 and 0.5 million years ago.

9.1 Fossil sites

Although *Homo erectus* was first recorded from Java in Indonesia, the fossils with the earliest dates are all from East Africa. This suggests that the migration of this species was from Africa to Asia, a movement we should expect if the genus *Homo* had an African origin two million years ago. As there are no *Homo* fossils outside Africa with undisputed dates before one million years ago it is assumed that a late *H. habilis* or early *erectus* achieved this migration in the early **Pleistocene**. However, there were most probably return migrations for the different races and forms of man with superior cultures and technology would have spread and conquered, or mixed with their fellows, in a complex of advancing waves.

In the Upper Bed II at Olduvai and at Koobi Fora, at a concordant date of 1.6 Ma, *Homo erectus* fossils and tools are first found. The appearance of this species, possibly by migration into the area is suddenly heralded by the appearance of stone tools of a new and different type. These **Acheulian hand-axes** are described later in this chapter. All the East African fossils with *H. erectus* features fall within a period from 1.5 Ma to the relatively recent date of 0.2 Ma, just 200 000 years ago. The most complete skull specimen is ER 3733 from Koobi Fora. Further north in Africa *Homo erectus* is found in Chad, Algeria and Morocco.

Figure 9.1   *Homo erectus*, a reconstruction by Z. Burian

The Trinil Java man is now dated at 0.7 Ma and although there are some possibly older specimens good dates for them are lacking. However, recent excavations at Djetis have revealed what appears to be a more massive-toothed earlier hominid remarkably like *H. habilis* (OH 13). That hominisation should have proceeded in parallel between Java and East Africa should not surprise us, nor indeed should gene flow over 10000 miles. Although Java is an island today it would have been part of the Asian mainland in the early Pleistocene.

In other parts of Asia later sites are known. The oldest in China is at Lan-t'ien at 0.7 Ma. These people were smaller-brained than the later Pekin Man whose remains, from **Choukoutien** near **Pekin** were first described in 1927. Excavation there was superbly done by Franz Weidenreich and Chinese colleagues but many of the remains were lost in the 1939–45 war, leaving only casts. In this collection there were a dozen skulls, several mandibles, 150 teeth and many post-cranial bones. Although Pekin man's tool technology was primitive they had domesticated fire and had clearly come to grips with the rigours of the first, **Günz, glaciation**.

The European *Homo erectus* fossils, such as the Mauer mandible or **Heidelburg jaw**, from Germany (0.35 Ma) are very rudimentary but clearly belonged to successful late members of the lineage that hunted in early Ice-Age

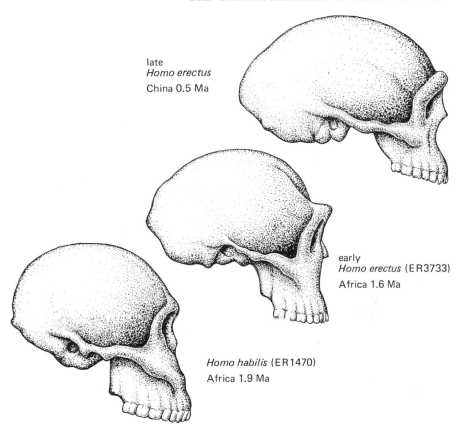

late
Homo erectus
China 0.5 Ma

early
Homo erectus (ER3733)
Africa 1.6 Ma

Homo habilis (ER1470)
Africa 1.9 Ma

Figure 9.2   Transition from *Homo habilis* to *Homo erectus*

Europe. They cannot have found these northern latitudes easy but the living sites revealed by archaeologists at **Torralba** (0.4 Ma) and **Ambrona**, in Northern Spain, and at **Terra Amata**, near Nice in France, testify to their successful hunting in a European climate colder than that of today. The **Petralona skull** from Greece at 500 000 years old shows the first signs of phyletic evolution, that last short step, to *Homo sapiens*.

9.2   The characteristics of *Homo erectus*

Homo erectus was skeletally fully modern, somewhat bigger than *H. habilis*, standing from 5 to 6 feet tall (1.5–1.8 m). However, the skeletal bone is different, for the outer cortex is thicker in all the skeletal remains. This robustness would be expected if the transition from *habilis* to *erectus* was to be achieved by an increased, allometric, growth in body size. Whilst some of the African skeletal remains indicate fully modern height there is no doubt that Pekin man was short and strong, with a chunky muscular build and reduced surface area to body ratio, that would have aided body-heat retention in a cold temperate climate. It is the skull of *erectus* that is so different from our own. The cranium was much flattened on top, the crown running forward into a

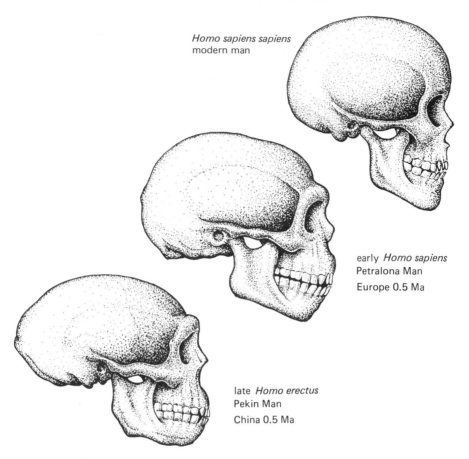

Homo sapiens sapiens
modern man

early *Homo sapiens*
Petralona Man
Europe 0.5 Ma

late *Homo erectus*
Pekin Man
China 0.5 Ma

Figure 9.3   Transition from *Homo erectus* to *Homo sapiens sapiens*

shelving down forehead which rose up and forwards into massive **brow-ridges** above the eyes. Viewed from above the head was anterio-posteriorly elongated; the **occipital** region at the back had a characteristic bump, a feature which persisted in later neanderthal man. The teeth and jaws were more massive than our own yet the face flatter and the jaw less prognathous. The brow-ridges buttressed and strengthened the face and, with the **zygomatic arch**, provided support at the side of the skull for large chewing muscles, for *Homo erectus*' diet was certainly unrefined by our standards. Although the head was held fully upright, the atlas vertebra joint to the skull, the **condylar articulation**, was not right under the cranium's centre of gravity but further back. To stop the head from hanging forward, massive **nuchal muscles** were inserted on the back of the *H. erectus* skull. In life, this would have concealed the posterior bump on the skull in the thick and wide musculature of the neck. Cranial volumes of early Java specimens are in the *H. habilis* range of 600–800 cm³. This enlargement must partly reflect an allometric increase in stature, but the mean of the species, 880 cm³, reflects a considerable increase in volume and complexity (see Appendix 2).

9.3 Cultural evolution

Homo erectus marks perhaps the most accelerated phase in hominisation from 1.5 to 0.5 Ma. Changes were not solely biological but very much cultural as well. Were we able to go back a million years we should probably find early man in bands of about 30 individuals, feeding largely on gathered plant materials brought to a home base or going out in tight-knit bands scavenging meat from the kills of large carnivores and beginning to hunt quarry for the first time. Tools would have been made from chosen local stones, from well-know localities, and no doubt some means devised of carrying water in skins or ostrich shells, so making some longer journeys possible to another needed resource. Spoken language would have been rudimentary, yet it would have been a major cohesive force used to establish order in the community, convey information and express ideas. Children would have slowly absorbed their culture by instructions received, by learning for themselves and imitating others in the social group.

At first sight these cultural features, such as a language, seem closely interwoven with a biological reality, like a language centre in the brain, but a clear distinction must be made between these two. **Cultural evolution** is fundamentally different in kind from biological evolutionary change. A definition of culture is given here to make clear this distinction: 'Culture is a store of information and set of behaviour patterns, transmitted, not by genetical inheritance, but by learning, by imitation, by instruction or by example.'

Culture is not a solely human realm. Many higher animals have transmitted culture of a simple kind, but what began with man as a largely biological evolutionary story ends with a predominantly cultural one. What made *Homo erectus* so successful was his society and upbringing, his cultural milieu, to a greater extent than would have been the case for a robust australopithecine at the same time. What also distinguishes *Homo erectus*, and particularly modern man, is that the ability to acquire that culture successfully and transmit it depends upon genetically inherited abilities. Thus although cultural transmission is different from genetic transmission and hence cultural evolution is distinct from organic evolution, biological fitness for cultural transmission is an essential part of cultural evolution.

9.4 Stone tools

The use of stone tools marks the beginning of a cultural stage in evolution that leads by steps over thousands of years to our modern industrial technology. From the time of early *Homo* the physical ability to make tools, the brain–hand–eye coordination and control improved. This was the biological evolution component. So too did the design of tools improve, the selection of materials for them, the methods of their manufacture and the diverse uses to which they were put. This was the cultural component.

Oldowan culture

Perhaps as early as 2.5 Ma *Homo habilis* purposively modified pebble tools for food preparation. The very earliest stone tools are barely recognisable as such,

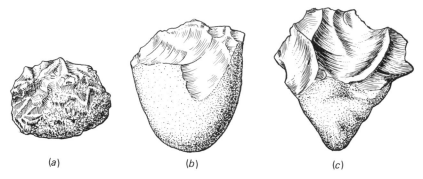

Figure 9.4   Tools of the Oldowan culture
(a) Quartz spheroid from Olduvai Gorge, Tanzania
(b) Basalt pebble tool, Oldowan chopper, from Olduvai
(c) Flint chopping tool from Clacton-on-Sea, Essex

but where a sedimented lake bed deposit contains concentrations of cobble-sized stones in a manner unlikely to have occurred by water-borne action, the suspicions of the archaeologist are aroused. The **Oldowan culture** takes its name from Olduvai. Any stone-tool culture with artefacts made up predominantly of cobble-sized stones from which a few flakes have been struck off, by blows with a hammer stone, to give a hand-held **Oldowan chopper** is characteristic. The early Oldowan tool-kit is composed of choppers and hammer stones, often of igneous basalt rock, and the chipped-off **percussion flakes** that might be used as scrapers. This culture was developed by *Homo habilis* and was taken to Asia by the earliest *habilis/erectus* men for it is found at its most developed in the culture of Pekin man. In Britain the earliest known stone culture, the **Clactonian**, named after Clacton in Essex, is of this type and probably dates from 0.4 Ma. No fossils accompany the Clactonian finds, but by this late stage the tools must have been made by *Homo erectus*.

Acheulian culture

The **Acheulian culture**, the Lower Palaeolithic hand-axe tradition, is first found at 1.6 Ma in East Africa, but there are possibly even earlier evidences of a hand-axe culture in Israel, so the culture may not have an African origin. The culture is named after **Saint-Acheul**, near Amiens, where it reached its peak 0.2 Ma ago. In Africa the earliest hand axes appear together with *Homo erectus* fossils at 1.6 Ma at both Olduvai and Koobi Fora. The Acheulian hand axe is not unlike the shape of an open flat hand. Made with the symmetry and the same size and thickness of a hand, this tool may have had some **third hand symbolism**. With its two flat sides and two cutting edges that lead to a point, these **bifaces** are more difficult to make than an Oldowan chopper. When held in the hand along one edge and around the rounded end, the other edge may be used as a chopping or slicing blade. The Acheulian tool-kit also comprised stone choppers, chisels, scrapers, cleavers, awls, anvils and hammer stones. However, the symmetrical hand-shaped biface is the key tool and the one requiring most skill to make.

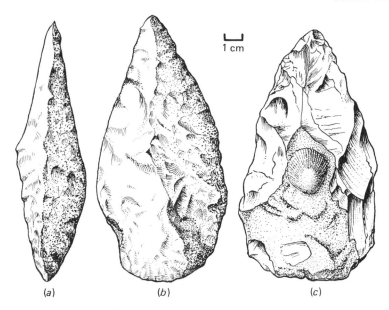

1 cm

(a)   (b)   (c)

Figure 9.5 Acheulian hand axes
(a) Early Acheulian phonolite hand axe, made by *H. erectus*, from Bed II Olduvai (edge profile view)
(b) as above (face view)
(c) Late Acheulian flint hand axe, made by *H. sapiens*, incorporating a fossil shell in its design (West Tofts, Norfolk)

Experimental archaeology

Stone tools and their use raise many questions about cultural evolution, some of which can be answered by an experimental approach to archaeology in which hypotheses are tested against each other with respect to the evidence gleaned from sites, where tools and fossil bones may together litter the floor of presumed living sites or home bases. Glyn Isaac, from Berkeley California, has been particularly concerned with sites at Koobi Fora that are over 1.5 million years old. He wished to be sure that his interpretations were not over subjective, for these sites are one hundred times older than the upper levels of the Palaeolithic, which was 15 000 years ago and which is still in the stone-age! He collected and mapped not only tools, but every stone flake and fossil bone fragment he could find, and meticulously attempted to reassemble them. This laborious exercise resulted in the reconstruction of some complete stones so that the sequence in which flakes were struck off could be determined and the places on the site where this was done demonstrated. This study and the study of percussion fractures of antelope bones proved objectively and beyond doubt that these assemblages of stones and bones were indeed on butchering sites and were not random geological events. At Olduvai, Peter Jones of Oxford has collected from the nearby basalt and phonolite formations, rocks of identical mineral composition to those of the bedded tools of Acheulian culture at the same site. By experiment, it took him more than two months to learn how to make similar hand axes with ease and accuracy. The **basalt** and

phonolite material was tough and large swinging follow-through blows were needed to chip off the secondary trimming flakes that give the tool its edge. In butchering goats, Jones found that the small flakes were only any use in making skin incisions, being hard to hold and blunting easily, but the hand axe with its weight and fair edge could skin, joint and gut almost like a knife. His hand-axes took five minutes to make and the primary cutting edge of the sharper phonolite tools could, if blunted, be resharpened by retouching with lighter flaking blows. Such studies of the materials used by early man for making his tools show how selective and how perceptive of the nature of the materials he was.

It is still not clear whether the co-existence of the 'developed Oldowan B' culture side-by-side for half a million years with Acheulian sites at Olduvai represents two tribal cultures or two types of site in different environments. It is probable that the Oldowan B sites are lakeside and the Acheulian ones game-butchering sites away from the lake. This second hypothesis is still not exclusive of the first, favoured by Mary Leakey, that two races of man shared the same environment in different ecological niches.

9.5   The hunting hypothesis

It is now thought that the litter of crunched and broken animal bones that were found by Raymond Dart in association with *Australopithecus africanus*, at Makapansgat, were in fact leopard kills. The relatively defenceless gracile australopithecine was part of the carnage. However, Dart built on his interpretations a novel hypothesis that these early hominids began hunting game animals. In the absence of any stone tools associated with this species this now seems improbable, but the hypothesis that hunting was a cultural spur to human evolution is valid. We know that chimpanzees are facultative carnivores, for they will occasionally catch small animals, especially the young of baboons or antelopes. This behaviour is only very occasional and in one case of chimpanzee cannibalism of an infant, in the wild, may have been brought on by dietary monotony at the time. We should regard some meat eating as an early probability in human evolution; certainly once hunting developed the social skills and demands on stamina would have been a powerful selective force, but this is unlikely to have got underway without the level of technology seen in *Homo erectus*. The protein food value of game meat needs no emphasis and may have been critically important in early *Homo* diets for adequate foetal and infant brain development. It is interesting in this respect that large numbers of small game-bird bones are found in Olduvai deposits. However, relative to the effort applied in pursuit of small game, group cooperation in the hunting of large herbivores would bring greater rewards in supplies of meat. The approximate number and density of herbivorous game mammals inhabiting an area of African savannah, with light woodland and lakeside, is known from present-day African National Parks.

Assuming that a group of hominids with a three mile radius home range lived in this environment, the numbers of animals in their range and their standing crop biomass may be calculated. Taking the data in Table 9.1, an annual cropping of only 1% of such a resource would supply each of 50 hominids with

Table 9.1 Game animals available as a food resource to a hominid band

Ungulate species	Approximate number of individuals	Estimated standing crop biomass
Buffalo	910	For a three mile radius
Hippopotamus	590	home-range (73.23 km²)
Elephant	125	with biomass at 250 kg ha^{-1}
Antelopes	955	= 1830 tonnes
	———	live weight
	2580	=915 tonnes
	———	butchered

(*from F. Bouliere 1959 and R.M. Laws 1969*)

half a kilogram of meat every day, a very generous ration. But such a resource would be hard to tap even if attractive. There is no good reason yet advanced, given the vegetable diet ancestry of apes, to suppose that *Homo erectus* was more carnivorous than ourselves; gathered fruits and seeds are likely to have been nutritionally more important in the diet. At Choukoutien, Pekin man evidently ate deer but also, judging from seed remains, large amounts of gathered wild fruits and berries. Scavenging from the kills of large carnivores is an entrée to hunting. Driving off lions and hyaenas could be achieved by group cooperation and once that skill was established, imitation of the lions' stalking and pincer movement tactics could have been successful. Some early competition with the carnivores of the savannah seems probable and many interesting comparative studies have been made of the hunting and scavenging behaviour of wild dogs, hyaenas and lions. Of the earliest evidences for mans' hunting skill, the site at Torralba, in Spain, is the most impressive. Here, at a date of 0.4 Ma, a steep-sided valley and marshy gully was used as a funnel trap for large game driven into it by bands of men using fire. On one small site the remains of 30 elephants, 25 horses, 25 deer, 10 wild cattle and 6 rhinoceros have been found, together with cleavers, hand axes and a litter of tool flakes. This must represent a permanent and regularly used butchery trap.

The hypothesised **benefits of hunting** to the hominisation process can be enumerated:

1 It places a high premium on cooperation between individual males and would thus reinforce social organisation.
2 The travelling and carrying would have put a strong selective pressure on effective bipedalism.
3 Catching and killing requires intelligence, ingenuity and technological skills. This has positive feedback to reinforce brain development and cultural development.
4 Food sharing would strengthen the whole social group and reinforce the home base.

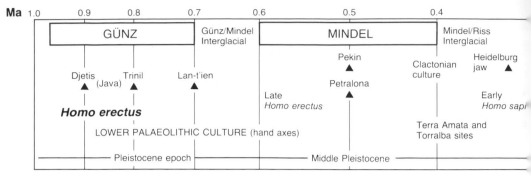

Ma 1.0   0.9   0.8   0.7   0.6   0.5   0.4

| GÜNZ | Günz/Mindel Interglacial | MINDEL | Mindel/Riss Interglacial |

Pekin ▲

Clactonian culture

Heidelburg jaw ▲

Djetis ▲ (Java)   Trinil ▲   Lan-t'ien ▲

Petralona ▲

Late *Homo erectus*

Early *Homo sapi*

Homo erectus

LOWER PALAEOLITHIC CULTURE (hand axes)

Terra Amata and Torralba sites

Pleistocene epoch ———— Middle Pleistocene ————

5 Speech would become an increasingly important part of planning and executing a hunt and discussion of the reported events of the hunt would be part of the group activity at butchery and feasting.

6 The resulting geographical knowledge would confer survival advantages and be an incentive to species dispersal and hence adoption of novel environments.

7 Pursuit in the chase was most probably the spur to the considerable human sweat gland development and perhaps evolution of body nakedness.

Nakedness

There are innumerable theories to account for human nakedness. Probably no single one alone is correct, but the aquatic evolutionary stage theory, sexual selection theory and sweat cooling theory have the greatest plausibility. Tropical early hominids would have been sparsley haired and black skinned, to be adapted to the heat and intense solar radiation. Modern apes and man have equal numbers of hairs but human hair on the body is extremely fine and short. Hunting would have involved periods of intense exertion and great metabolic heat production. Only with an efficient cooling system, and yet head covering of hair to insulate the brain from the radiation effects of the sun, could temperature regulation be achieved. Black skin absorbs radiant heat and this too must have favoured some efficient cooling system. Man does not pant like most hot mammals but has several million sweat glands instead, at densities up to 500 cm^{-2} of skin. Body sweat secretion, at rates of up to 1.6 litres hour^{-1}, can, in dry air, produce evaporative cooling effects of 3.6 MJ hour^{-1}. This one kilowatt cooling system would have worked better from a sparsely haired skin, with rich blood supply regulated by vasodilatation and constriction. Whereas there is evidence for early man's hunting there is as yet no hard evidence of an **aquatic ancestry** stage. This hypothesis, put forward by Sir Alistair Hardy and recently developed in a popular account by Elaine Morgan, relates not only to reduction of body hair but also to many other hominid features of interest and their ideas should be cautiously entertained. Certainly great water dependence and lakeside living are proven. Desmond Morris makes a good case for **sexual selection** being involved in hair loss; this is a subjective but nonetheless real view for modern man, where the physical attributes of skin and hair (so played on by the cosmetics manufacturers) play a part in mate selection by males. Few

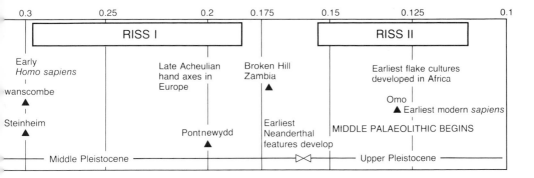

people would deny that they are influenced by the **epigamic**, or sexual signal, characteristics of the opposite sex. Once man became naked, skin and hair adornment were quite probably adopted as display features. Red ochre tablets are known from Terra Amata at 0.3 Ma. The cultural significance of colour to primitive man is shown by the fact that Australian aborigines have been known to travel 300 miles to acquire red ochre, for body adornment, from a distant mine.

Fire

Fire has been a natural feature of tropical savannah grasslands for sufficiently long for many plant and animal forms to be adapted to it. Both volcanic events and lightning strikes can cause fires and these may burn extensively in dry seasons. Early man undoubtedly increased the frequency of fires in such environments for open grassland favours the highest carrying capacity of herbivorous game animals. The earliest fire hearths are hard to pin-point. There is a charred ground living-site at 2.5 Ma near Lake Turkana. Certainly by 1.0 Ma there was fire in use in the caves of southern France and fire hearths are present from the lowest occupation levels of the Choukoutien cave at 0.5 Ma, and was used at Torralba at 0.4 Ma for driving herds of game into the gully. Not only would fire have been used for warmth and frightening prey, but also for that peculiarly human activity, cooking. Edmund Leach, the social anthropologist, believes that cooking was not just a biological necessity, that destroyed pathogens and softened food, but became a symbolic act or **ritual** which transformed the food into something clean and safe and different from its former nature. Thus fire became a tool, but one of special cultural significance. *Focus*, the latin word for the fire place, still retains its meaning in our language. The bright, warm, beast-defying fire was the fore-gathering centre of the home base, in the dark wild nights of prehistory.

10 The hunter-gatherers: *Homo sapiens*

Modern hunter-gatherers such as Aborigines, Amazon Indians and Bushmen are the last practitioners of a way of life universally followed by primitive man. *Homo erectus* was a **hunter-gatherer** and so too were our *Homo sapiens* ancestors until the beginning of the Neolithic era. The phyletic evolution from one species to the other was a short step in biological evolution, completing the hominisation process. But culturally enormous changes have overtaken man in the past 300 000 years. These have been changes which by their very nature seem to impel the rate of change at an ever-increasing pace. Man has been for the longest period of his history a hunter-gatherer. This is the way of life to which we are biologically adapted, yet few men today continue such a seemingly precarious existence. It is important to realise that many of the social and technological foundations of our modern society were initiated in this late stone age period.

10.1   Phyletic hominisation

In 1959 a new and important fossil skull was unearthed in Greece, at **Petralona**. Dated at 0.5 Ma, the same date as Pekin man, it is a skull so markedly unlike the heavy-browed *Homo erectus* as to be regarded as an uncomfortable fit in that species. On the other hand it foreshadows the **Steinheim** and **Swanscombe** skulls which, dated at about 0.3 Ma, are much younger and are regarded as early *Homo sapiens*. The Petralona skull has a brain volume of 1200 cm^3, a slightly higher vaulted skull, reduced brow ridges, reduced bone thickness and smaller teeth of a less robust kind, when compared with *Homo erectus*. (In that it fits exactly between the two species it may be considered as evidence for phyletic gradualism in evolution.) To us, Steinheim man and Swanscombe man (early *Homo sapiens*) would still appear facially primitive, with heavy jaws, thick necks and long skulls, but they do manifest a further stage in the hominisation process. For although there are ill-defined racial groupings of modern man they all have in common lighter jaws and teeth, higher vaulted crania, foreheads without marked brow ridges, thinner necks and a markedly reduced bone thickness, and hence mass, of the entire skeleton. Figure 10.1 expresses the final biological evolution of forms of *Homo sapiens*. There is general agreement amongst anthropologists that the species has arisen in a **polyphyletic** manner, several lines leading to the different geographical races. Yet it is thought that gene flow and migration between geographical races has been at least as important as phyletic hominisation within a line. The diagonal genetic movement expressed by this schematic figure has certainly ensured the maintenance of a single global gene pool, yet there are physical similarities which link vertical phyletic lines equally strongly. Although this chapter concentrates on the Neanderthals and

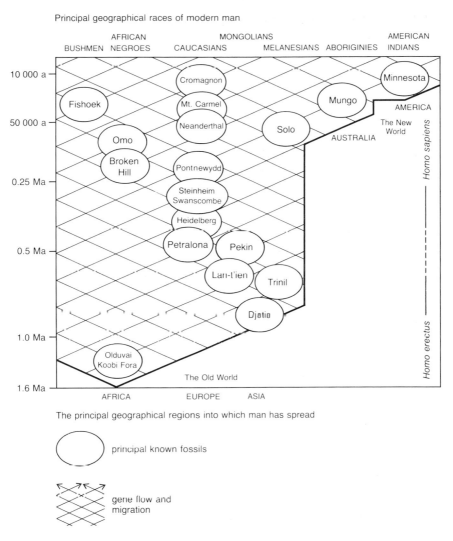

Principal geographical races of modern man

AFRICAN   MONGOLIANS   AMERICAN
BUSHMEN NEGROES   CAUCASIANS   MELANESIANS ABORIGINIES   INDIANS

10 000 a — Cromagnon — Minnesota

Fishoek — Mt. Carmel — Mungo — AMERICA

50 000 a — Neanderthal — Solo — The New World — AUSTRALIA

Omo — *Homo sapiens*

Broken Hill — Pontnewydd

0.25 Ma — Steinheim Swanscombe

Heidelberg

Petralona — Pekin

0.5 Ma

Lan-t'ien — Trinil

Djetio

1.0 Ma — *Homo erectus*

Olduvai Koobi Fora

The Old World

1.6 Ma

AFRICA   EUROPE   ASIA

The principal geographical regions into which man has spread

◯ principal known fossils

gene flow and migration

Figure 10.1   The final biological evolution of modern man
The principal known fossils are placed on a time axis according to geographical location. (See text.)

inhabitants of Western Asia and Europe in the Upper Palaeolithic an equivalent hominisation has continued as a broad progression throughout the world in the last million year span.

10.2   *Homo sapiens* from the ice ages

Europe and Asia have experienced quite drastic climatic changes over the past million years as the ice sheets have expanded and retreated with each of the glaciations. Not only did these geological events scour the surfaces of the land, but at each advance they also often obliterated the early traces of man. Only in caves and in certain lake beds and alluvial deposits have these recent human fossil bones been found. Because these are often only single specimens the picture is fragmentary, though tools and very durable artefacts may be preserved. Many of the remains of wood, fibre and skin have rotted away, a fact that may bias interpretation. One should not either be misled by the common name for our species in calling these fossils men. It is probable, for example, that both Steinheim man and Swanscombe man were women! The Lower Palaeolithic came to an end with the late Acheulian cultures reaching their peak just before the onset of the **Riss glaciations**. What became of the earliest *Homo sapiens* (Swanscombe) types we do not know, but they do show affinities with the specialised Neanderthal race as well as later modern man. The human molar and child's jaw fragment recently discovered at Pontnewydd cave, in Wales, (dated at 250 000a) show primitive Neanderthal features.

The Neanderthals have for a long time fascinated students of prehistory. Their distinctive stone culture appears for the first time in Europe after the long fossil gap of the Riss glaciations at 75 000 a (0.075 Ma). They developed a sophistication in stone working that gave them cultural dominance in Europe until after the close of the second **Wurm glaciation** at 35 000 a. Not only was their culture new but their physical form was different, an undoubted adaptation to the rigours of survival in such cold times. For this latter reason they are regarded as a subspecies.

10.3   Neanderthal man, *Homo sapiens neanderthalensis*

The Valley of the **Neander River** (Neanderthal) is near Dusseldorf in Germany. Here in 1856 some remains were found in a limestone cave, which initially excited only local curiosity. Between 1866 and 1910, however, many more European cave sites revealed the remains of primitive man, and in the atmosphere of acceptance of Darwinism, the **Neanderthals** gained a popular image of being more primitive than we see them today. Often, in early works, they are portrayed as hunched and stooping with massively robust and hairy limbs – the classical cartoon caveman. This image was largely due to a failure to interpret correctly one particular skeleton as being that of an elderly arthritic man; they were as upright and un-apelike as we are. The classic Neanderthal from the early Würm glaciation was stocky, powerfully muscular with large joints and hands. The skulls were distinctive, being long and low

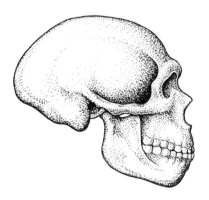
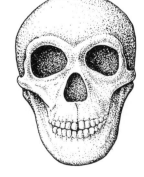

Figure 10.2   *Homo sapiens neanderthalensis*

domed, like those of *Homo erectus*; but only moderately brow-ridged and of much larger cranial volume. So far as brain size is concerned their mean volume was greater than that of modern man, a fact which may reflect the need to control more musculature than we posses. The jaws are robust with a molar gap between the last molar, the wisdom tooth, and the ascending branch of the jaw bone. There is a ridged **occipital** protruberance at the back of the skull with below it a larger area for **nuchal** (neck) muscle attachment than in modern man. One feature of interest is the much enlarged nasal cavity: Neanderthals are often portrayed with broad and bulbous noses. Such a physiological adaptation, in their arctic climate, would have conserved both heat and moisture in the freezing air. It is worth noting that the elk (moose), saiga antelope and reindeer, all hunted by Neanderthals, have relatively larger nasal cavities than ungulates from more temperate regions.

We know more of the Neanderthal way of life than of any previous type of man. That they had a greater level of human consciousness is shown by the fact that they were the first people to bury their dead, for the act of **ritualised burial** indicates an awareness of the personal significance of death to the mourners. At Shanidar Cave, in Northern Iraq, a man, a woman and a child were buried together in a single rock-cleft grave. The grave soil contained evident plant remains and analysis has shown the presence of the pollen of six recognisable wild flower species, such as wild hollyhocks, gathered in the late spring 40 000 years ago. In contrast, evidence of cannibalism, which it is thought was earlier practised by Pekin man, still persisted amongst the Neanderthals. Grisly as this appears to us, cannibalism of the brain contents, scooped out through a manifestly enlarged foramen magnum, is best understood as a ritual of repossession of a lost spirit, or adoption of another's 'life force'. Other Neanderthals were buried with the symbolic skulls of large carnivores.

Neanderthals apparently made no ornaments for themselves and seemed not to use bone and antler tools as later Upper Palaeolithic man did. At burial sites such as those at **Le Moustier** in France, there are abundant evidences of what is thereby named the **Mousterian flake culture**. Flake cultures differ from the Acheulian hand-axe culture in that bladed flakes are struck from a core, whereas the hand-axe tool is the core stone from which flakes were struck. Secondly, only the finest flaking glass-like silicate minerals such as flint and obsidian were used and these were finely retouched to give a more effective edge. A large tabular block of flint was first obtained and struck with a single heavy blow to produce a conical core. From this core, flakes were struck off by single heavy blows to give very fine tools with razor-sharp edges. Retouching, a finer flaking of the cutting edge, was done by lighter percussion from a more elastic hammer such as a long bone or piece of hard wood. Mousterian **retouched flakes**, such as **side scrapers**, **notches**, **points** and **denticulates** would have been used for such things as skinning, sharpening sticks, fixing to spear points or as fine saws (see Fig. 10.3).

The Neanderthals were spread over much of Europe and Western Asia where the climate was like that of the present tundra biome. Although caves give us the best remains it is probable that tent shelters were more commonly

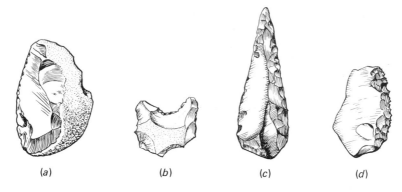

(a)   (b)   (c)   (d)

Figure 10.3 The Mousterian tool kit of Neanderthal man
(a) Sidescraper tool for skinning   (c) Point, spear head
(b) Notch tool, for stick sharpening   (d) Denticulate saw

used as the home base. Much detailed recent archaeology in the **Ukraine** USSR, has shown that these bands of hunters killed reindeer, wild horses, moose and musk-ox in the northern plains and wild sheep and deer in the south towards the Black Sea. Ukrainian sites are thought to have centred on large shelters, about nine metres wide and three metres in height, built of branches arching together and overlain with skins, and often weighted down with the bones of mammoths. Only bones, fire hearths and Mousterian flint tools remain to suggest what life was like for a hunting band of Neanderthals. Some notion of their clothing, for example, may be deduced from the initially puzzling fact that at excavated sites fox, wolf and hare skeletons are found without their foot bones. This might possibly mean that these animals were skinned with the feet left in the skin as ties for attachment. In confirmation of this plausible hypothesis no needles have been found which could have been used for sewing, but only the foot bones of those animals, grouped together inside the shelter, the skins having long since rotted away! How these people hunted and trapped so efficiently is still not known. It is presumed that the cave sites such as **Les Eyzies** and **Combe Grenal**, in France, were used seasonally, as here game mammals would have migrated north and south, to and from summer and winter grazing. Sun drying, smoking or freezing of this meat could have supplied them with protein needs between migrations, and the gathering of fruits and other plant foods would have been possible in summer to broaden their diet.

The appearance and disappearance of Neanderthal man

The Mousterian culture presumably arose from the late Oldowan and Acheulian cultures which preceded it. We do not know who brought the tool-flaking techniques to Europe, athough their earliest development seems to have been in South West Africa at the time of the Riss glaciation in Europe. Although the culture and the Neanderthals themselves took a long time to develop, their departure is fairly abrupt. At the close of the Würm II glaciation, after 40 000 years of Neanderthal predominance, these people and their

Mousterian culture suddenly seem to disappear like the ice sheets themselves. To the south less specialised Neanderthals were found. These are typified by the **Mount Carmel** finds, in Israel, in the cave of Mugharet es Skuhl, at 40 000 a. It is generally supposed that less specialised forms of *Homo sapiens* or more modern forms from Western Asia, or even Africa, moved north and west into Europe, for at 35 000 a. fully modern *Homo sapiens sapiens* remains are found. Why did the Neanderthals disappear? Three reasons are commonly advanced. First, their technology, though an improvement on the Acheulian, was far inferior to the stone working and skill displayed by Upper Palaeolithic man. Secondly, their heavy build and probably demanding nutritional requirements were not an advantage in the Mid-Würm interglacial. Thirdly, their sociocultural level was inferior to that of their successors whose jewellery, figurines and cave paintings mark the golden age of prehistory. From a genetical viewpoint it is possible to see how these people slowly underwent adaptive change and isolation over 50 000 years to become the neanderthaloid subspecies, but the evolved Neanderthal skull and skeletal features disappear from the fossil record more rapidly than could have occurred by selection alone in 5000 years. We must therefore assume that the change in human characteristics at this time is predominantly due to the arrival of *Homo sapiens sapiens* from elsewhere, though some Neanderthal genes may remain in our present day gene pool, as a result of interbreeding. Quite how they died out we shall never know.

10.4 The final biological evolution of *Homo sapiens sapiens*

The remaining biological changes to fully modern man occurred during this last ice age period. These involved a thinning and lightening of bones, a greater development of the vaulted cranium and steep forehead, reduced skull length and a further reduction of the jaws. As the teeth were bunched up closer in the jaw and drawn back under the face a more prominent chin developed. The gap between the last molar and ascending jaw branch closes and there is a definite tendency, still continuing today, for the last molars not to erupt, or to do so with too little room for comfort. This shift of physical character from *Homo erectus* to *Homo sapiens* has been described by evolutionary biologists as neotenous. **Neoteny** is the retention, in evolution, of some more characteristically juvenile feature in the adult form of a species. It is a common evolutionary development displayed by many groups of animals and as long ago as 1920 Louis Bolk suggested that this process of prolongation of juvenile features was centrally responsible for much of man's evolutionary transformation from the apes. Today the argument for neotony goes as follows: if certain juvenile characteristics are selectively favoured, their retention into adult life may occur by the genes that produce such features being reinforced or prolonged in their expression; at the same time, were those genes that are responsible for the more adult thick boned skull and skeleton less favoured by selection, such robust characteristics might diminish. Growth patterns are known to be governed by sets of genes and gene switches, turning on and off the genic system, which in their turn affect patterns and rates of growth, the latter often being mediated by hormones. Two pertinent examples of hormone-

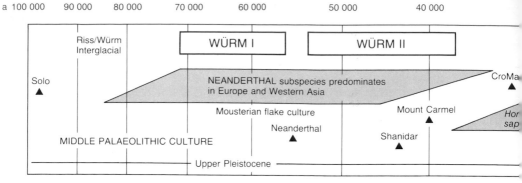

mediated changes will illustrate this. Melatonin, a hormone from the pineal body, influences the onset of puberty, whilst somatotrophin, the growth hormone, stimulates the growth of bone. The evolution of a large-brained, small-jawed form, with reduced body hair, light skeleton and late puberty can all be argued to be neotonous developments in our evolution, achieved by relatively minor genic modification.

How and why this selection for modern body form occurred is problematic. Cooking and tool developments would certainly reduce selection for powerful jaws whilst tool-use might reduce selection for massive individual strength. Perhaps sexual selection for more juvenile facial features, like the high forehead and small jaw, could have contributed to change. The physical difference between modern races is attributable to different genetic ancestry, different climatic and environmental adaptations and different cultural concepts of handsomeness and beauty upon which, respectively, natural and sexual selection have operated.

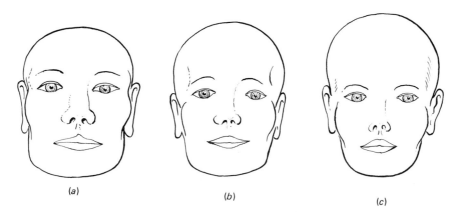

Figure 10.4   Neotenisation of the human face
From left to right jaw size decreases, but cranial height increases at the expense of cranial length. Relative nose size is also decreased.
(a) is based upon a Neanderthal skull, (b) on the Cro-Magnon skull, (c) shows a more juvenile face following this trend.

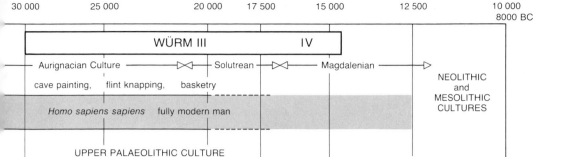

10.5 Cro-Magnon Man and the Upper Palaeolithic Culture

This final stage of human biological evolution is represented by many fossils from caves with Upper Palaeolithic artefacts. The type specimen is **Cro-Magnon Man**, dated at about 30 000 a, and coming from the Dordogne region of France. Taller and finer boned than the preceding Neanderthals they were skeletally little different from ourselves, having the neotenic skull features described in the previous section. Whilst the human skeleton has changed little in the past 30 000 years the same cannot be said for human culture which has changed dramatically. Three cultural epochs mark the **Upper Palaeolithic** of Western Europe, the **Aurignacian**, the **Solutrean** and the **Magdalenian**. It should be noted that many other late Palaeolithic cultures are found in other parts of the world. The last European cavemen had a very sophisticated culture, witnessed to by their impressive cave art at places such as **Lascaux**, in France, and **Altamira**, in Spain. Nobody seeing these art forms can fail to be moved by their sensitivity, executed skill and displayed imagination. Ritual burial sites reveal the development of jewelery; coloured beads and pierced teeth were strung together or stitched to skins and ivory bracelets were worn. Upper Palaeolithic tools are characterised by the very long flakes struck from a cylindrical core. This was done by indirect percussion with an antler-tine punch rested on the edge of the core block, which was then struck off by a hammer blow or by using a heavy chest pressure flaking staff with a pointed end (see Figure 10.6). The manufacture of more blades in less time and from less flint stone made this highly efficient. These long flakes were then retouched to make knives, saws and pointed chisel **burins**. Tiny flint points and barbs, the so called **microliths**, were also developed. These could be fitted to arrows and harpoons. The first use of the bow is hard to date, but it was certainly used in hunting in Upper Palaeolithic times. The survival of these people in the Third and Fourth Würm glaciations was even more impressive than that of their Neanderthal antecedents. This survival was possible because of their superior tool kits and technology, now utilising bone, antler and ivory as well as flint as the tool materials. The bow-drill, derived from the hunting bow, made possible the threading of beads and the development of bone needles for the stitching of skins. For the first time there is also evidence of basketry. Baskets must have greatly eased the gathering of fruits and nuts as well as providing better storage for gathered food.

87

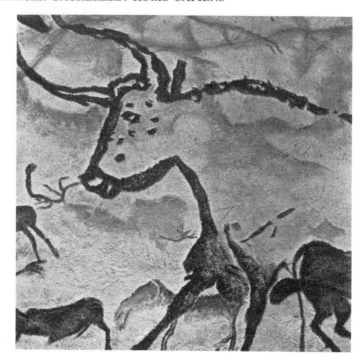

Figure 10.5   The Bull of Lascaux
Once hunted by Palaeolithic man, the fierce auroch (*Bos primigenius*) was domesticated in later Neolithic times. Wild cattle were hunted to extinction in historic times.

In Europe, at the close of the Würm glaciation just 15 000 years ago, there lived fully modern man of sophisticated yet still stone-age culture. This final stage of biological evolution is typified by Cro-Magnon man. Similar human evolutionary development occurred elsewhere. During the early Würm glaciation so great were the ice caps that the world's sea levels fell markedly. This made the water barrier between continents and islands less formidable, thus Australia was entered more than 30 000 years ago from South East Asia. Our reasons for believing this are that Australian aborigine fossil ancestors at Mungo, dated at 30 000 a, share physical features with early *Homo sapiens* from Solo in Java, dated at 100 000 a. Probably successive waves of Upper Palaeolithic peoples invaded the Australian continent, crossing the deep Straits of Timor by canoe. The early Mongoloids, whose Upper Palaeolithic culture mirrors that of Europe, crossed the frozen Bering Straits into Arctic North America 25 000 years ago to people the whole of pre-Columban America, from Greenland down to Tierra del Fuego. Rhodesian man, from Broken Hill in Zambia, had arguably neanderthaloid and primitive negroid features, but later Omo fossils are modern. In South Africa the skulls from Fishoek, at 30 000 a, are very like modern bushmen and hottentots. Since the last interglacial 35 000 years ago modern man has been one, racially diverse, single sub-species, *Homo sapiens sapiens*.

10.6   The operative efficiency of man

How should a biologist view the evolution of technology? Perhaps one view that will serve as a model in an assessment of the stone age is to consider man's **operative efficiency**: efficient use of resources and efficient use of energy. Material and energy resources are competed for by all plants and animals. In this man is no exception, but he brings an opportunistic and inventive nature to the competition.

Consider the first tool-use of a hammer stone by *Homo habilis*, to crack open a food item. First, the stone having more mass than his hand alone will give a blow more force. Secondly, by raising the stone up above his head, with one set of arm muscles, the stone is given potential energy. If it is then brought down by gravity its potential energy will become kinetic, but at the same time work done by the other muscles of the arm in propelling it down will add more energy to the blow. Both sets of antagonistic muscles, normally opposed to each other, have thus been used to apply one forceful blow. Their work has been summed. This exploitation of potential energy is utilised in later stone-age devices such as the bent-back sapling in a spring trap, the hunting bow and the deadfall trap, in which a log is hoisted into a tree to fall, when triggered, and noose an animal with great violence.

Consider tool sharpening. The energy expended in a blow, the mechanical work done, is clearly limited by the muscle power of the arm and its length. But the force applied to the struck object may be increased by reducing the area over which the energy is applied. A sharp tool can therefore cut skin and meat which no hands could tear apart. The hafting of a tool, such as a stone axe to a wooden handle, by effectively increasing arm length, increases the exploitation of potential energy in combination with this blade effect. A further principle is illustrated by saws. One problem with sharp blades is that they have large frictional blade surfaces and so tend to stick if used to cut deep. The saw, the denticulate edge of the retouched flake, is a different type of tool which solves this problem. A single notched edge may rip or tear only once at each stroke, but if serrated along all of its length the work done at each stroke is increased in proportion to the number of teeth in the edge. More work done per unit time is increased power for man.

Until the domestication of fire all human energy was derived from human muscle power alone, though solar power as heat for drying, etc. had its uses. **Extrasomatic energy sources** clearly gave man an increased capacity to exploit his environment. Fire was undoubtedly the first of these, providing heat, sterilisation of cooked food, extension of the day length, hardening of sticks and heat tempering of flints, the driving of game etc. The smoking of meat and laying-up of gathered food stores for winter gave man extrasomatic food reserves. Animal furs gave heat conservation. An even more sophisticated form of increased efficiency in energy and material harvesting is the exploitation of game migration routes. This effectively meant that the biological productivity of a much larger area is tapped at one point thus reducing the energy expenditure that would be involved in collecting from the whole game animals' range. **Economy in materials** is illustrated by the fact that a premium on the value of flint may have prompted the flake-blade culture

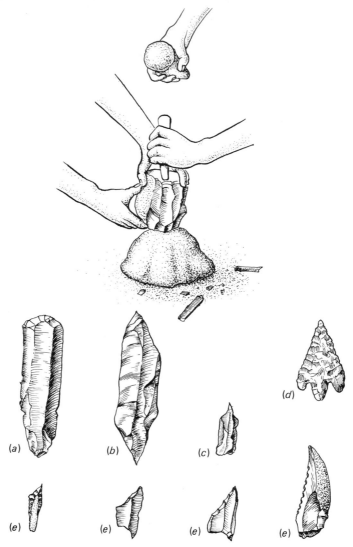

Figure 10.6 The Upper Palaeolithic tool kit of Cro-Magnon Man
Using a hammer stone and antler tine punch, long bladed flakes were struck from a flint core placed on a stone anvil. Flakes were then retouched to make such things as (a) end scraper, (b) burin chisel, (c) microburin drill, (d) arrowhead, (e) microliths (barbs).

of the Aurignacians. A kilogram flint core could be worked to yield 50 good blades with a total cutting edge length of 25 metres. This represents a tenfold efficiency increase on the Acheulian cultures. This feature of **opportunism**, seizing the best chance, working in tandem with the inventive skill of his brain gave to stone-age man his individual success. As culture picked up and passed on successes, the human species' power over its environment increased beyond the normal energy and physical limits for a hominid, so setting the scene for the dawn of agriculture and the earliest civilisations.

11 The origins of agriculture

About fifteen thousand years ago, that is about 13 000 BC, the last Würm glaciation came slowly to an end. During the glaciation ice sheets had covered up to one quarter of the Earth's surface and the deposited ice lay, as it still does in Greenland, up to 3 000 metres in thickness. The long thaw, which continued for several millenia (thousands of years) not only brought a rise in temperature but also increased sea levels. These in turn led to greater evaporation and increased rainfall. The plants and animals adapted to the temperate zone, once forced south by the ice-age, moved north again; cold arid tundras gave way to warm moist woodlands. The hunted herbivores such as reindeer and elk moved north to be replaced from the south by various species of deer and wild cattle in the lowlands and wild sheep and goats in the hills. The retreat of the ice allowed freer movement of isolated animals and plants, whose local population characteristics may have lead to new species formation, or on remeeting resulted in some **hybrid vigour**. Certainly, for man, new free migration may have resulted in an enrichment in human genetic diversity. In this last post-glacial epoch hunter-gatherers first settled to farming.

11.1 Neolithic and Mesolithic cultures

The term **Neolithic**, the New Stone Age, was originally defined by the artefacts discovered. In Northern Europe, such finds as the developed and decorated pottery and polished flint axes came to be associated with the early farming that was clearly practised by these people. But the Neolithic culture did not arise as soon as the ice retreated for there was an intervening transition period before it known as the Mesolithic or Middle Stone Age.

Today the **Mesolithic** is rather loosely defined as a post-glacial and yet pre-agricultural period in which the hunter-gatherers became more settled and more diversified as communities in relation to each other. They retained the sophisticated use of microliths for spears, harpoons and sickles developed in the Upper Palaeolithic; they evolved more sophisticated basketry and pottery and became less nomadic, that is more settled, and certainly not living in caves any more for most of the year, but constructing hut shelters in the open instead. Life was probably less harsh than during the ice age and there was evidently abundant game and especially good fishing. The rise in sea levels, to cover the present continental shelf around Britain, for example, meant that waters were rich in soil nutrients and there is evidence from the oyster shell kitchen middens, many feet thick, that these shellfish were a major dietary item. In Northern Europe, this **Maglemosian culture**, as it is called, is the predominant example of Mesolithic life. At **Star Carr** in Yorkshire, at a radio-carbon date of 7500 BC, excellent remains have been found of a lakeside seasonal camp in which wooden paddles, dugout canoes and hunting bows have been preserved together with microliths of flint and tools of bone and antler.

The Mesolithic is, however, an ill-defined period for the Near East, where Old World farming began around 9 000 BC, the Upper Palaeolithic shades almost imperceptibly into the Neolithic. In Britain the Mesolithic continued beyond the fifth millenium BC, that is until the Neolithic people, or their culture, spread the practice of farming to these shores. But in each area of the world the story of cultural evolution is obviously different. Thus in most of Africa, south of Egypt, the Mesolithic existed only as a waterside fishermans culture from 8 000 BC onwards, the Late Stone Age making a transition into the early Iron Age from the first century BC. Rather than fit cultural evolutionary events to strict divisions (like Upper Palaeolithic, Mesolithic and Neolithic) contemporary archaeologists feel that it is better to describe the way of life of the people concerned and to distinguish the diversity of culture and methods of subsistence that existed at a particular time. The earliest **domestications** of plants and animals began very soon after the last ice age. Where this first started in the Near East, in a small nuclear region, the culture although only Upper Palaeolithic or early Mesolithic has been termed **Proto-Neolithic** to distinguish it from the Mesolithic that continued elsewhere. When settled farming was developed by more and more people, the culture of those with these new tried methods can be described as typically **Neolithic**.

11.2 The nuclear region of the Near East

At the end of the last century, Alphonse de Candolle suggested, without any archaeological evidence, that the origin of agriculture was in the Near East, where grasses clearly related to modern wheat and barley grew wild. The occurence of wild sheep and goats in this area lent strength to the hypothesis. Although interest in the ancient civilisations of Babylon and Egypt, at the edge of this area, was intense a century ago it has only been in the last fifty years that evidence has been forthcoming to prove that the Near Eastern geographical area was the principal centre for the origins of agriculture in the Old World.

In the Eastern Mediterranean the coastal countries of Israel, Lebanon, Syria and Southern Turkey form one climatic zone, the **Levant**, influenced by the Mediterranean Sea. These areas receive a regular winter rainfall and have hot dry summers. Further to the north, the **Taurus Mountains** of Turkey and, round to the south east, the **Zagros Mountains** of Iran form a range with flanking foothills and plateaus and have a regular winter rainfall and the same hot dry summers. These uplands drain towards the south west into the great Tigris and Euphrates rivers which empty into the Persian Gulf, at present-day Basra, close to the ancient city of Babylon.

To the south of the whole area are deserts. The present-day countries of Israel, Jordan, Syria, Lebanon, Turkey, Iraq and Western Iran thus constitute a centre where many of the earliest domestications are believed to have occurred. James Breasted (1916) first described the Nile delta, Levant and **Mesopotamia** (literally between rivers region of the Tigris and Euphrates) as the **Fertile Crescent**, being the presumed area where early agriculture and

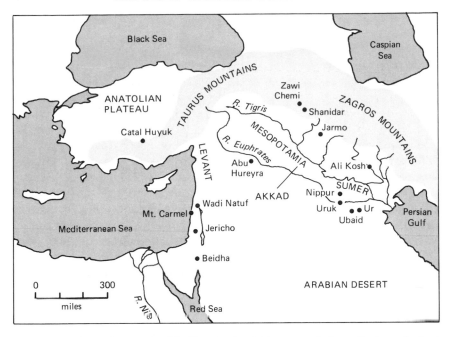

Figure 11.1 The nuclear region of the Near East in which many early domestications of animals and plants occurred and in which agriculture first gave rise to civilisation

civilisation began. But today we believe that it is probably to the north of the crescent in the Taurus and Zagros range of foothills that most early domestications occurred. Robert Braidwood (1967) regards this as the **nuclear zone** for it corresponds most closely to the habitat requirements of the first domesticated species.

11.3 The Proto-Neolithic culture of the Natufians

In a cave in the **Wadi Natuf** of Galilee, excavations in 1927 first revealed the remains of a culture that predominated in the whole of this now desert area. Between 11 000 BC and 8 000 BC, such **Natufian** sites are found at Jericho in the deepest layers of the city, on Mount Carmel, at 'Ain Mallaha in the Jordan Rift and at Abu Hureyra in Syria. The Natufians were not farmers but they had made some important first steps and can be described as **incipient agriculturalists**. First, these sites contain trace carbonised remains of many wild cereal seeds such as einkorn wheat and the natural tetraploid hybrid emmer wheat, as well as two-rowed barley. Secondly, there are many sickles, made from deer antlers, grooved to take a series of microlith blades. The microwear sheen of these blades, studied under the microscope, shows that they were used for cutting siliceous grass stems. Pestles, mortars, basalt and limestone grinding stones and stone storage bins in the ground of the hut sites indicate that the harvested cereal grains were processed and a considerable surplus stored. Jack Harlan, an agricultural archaeologist, has studied the almost pure stands of wild **einkorn** wheat that still grow in certain upland Near East habitats, the stands being almost as dense as a cultivated wheat field. By experiment he

Figure 11.2   Antler sickle fitted with flint blades used by the Natufians to harvest grain on Mount Carmel

found that he could gather by hand alone 1 kg of edible grain per hour. He increased his rate 20% by using a Natufian sickle. Wild einkorn grows on rocky hills and he estimated that altitudinal differences would have extended the natural harvest period to at least three weeks. In this time alone a family could gather most of their annual carbohydrate needs without tilling, sowing or domestication changes to the wild species. Although the Natufians were fairly settled people, on account of their milling and storage technology, they also relied on fishing, hunting and mollusc-eating for animal protein. There is no evidence of any animal domestication though herds of deer and gazelles may have been followed in hunting and perhaps protected for the first time from other predators.

Zawi Chemi and Shanidar Cave

Contemporary with these Natufian sedentary grain collectors of the Levant, the new occupants of the once-Neanderthal **Shanidar Cave** in Northern Iraq were beginning to domesticate the wild sheep of the Zagros Mountains. The Shanidar cave itself was perhaps now only used in winter, but at **Zawi Chemi**, nearby, are the remains of a classical Proto-Neolithic village dated at 9 000 BC. Evidence indicates that the people depended upon gathered wheat, legumes, acorns and pistachio nuts. Wild pigs, cattle, sheep, deer and goats were all hunted, but the bones of young sheep are particularly abundant and many archaeologists interpret this as being due to selective culling from a large tended herd. Zawi Chemi has the bones of dogs which are physically distinguishable from those of a wolf. The usefulness of such domesticated dogs could only have been in hunting originally, but their presence in this situation may signify their use in herding for the first time.

11.4   Farming begins

It is important at this point to be clear what we mean by such words and phrases as agriculture, food production and domestication. A farming system dependent upon domesticated plants and animals has four component activities (Redman 1978):

1. **propagation** – a purposive breeding of animals or sowing of seeds;
2. **husbandry** – a care of growing animals and growing plants;
3. **harvesting** – the collection of the food resources that were propagated and husbanded;
4. **conservation** – the retention of a reservoir of selected seed and animals to breed from.

With such a system the earliest farmers must have anticipated an increased yield by their propagation, husbandry, and conserving efforts, or they would have stuck to the hunter-gatherer life and just got on with the harvesting alone! The farmers' perception of increased yields, or at least increased ease of harvesting, must also have persisted for a long time, for once farming began the cultivated species themselves altered their biological adaptations to suit the farming process to which they were subjected. The animals and plants, in other words, evolved by **artificial selection** into domesticated species. The characteristics of these domesticated species and their importance to human evolution are dealt with later in this chapter.

It is important to ask ourselves why these perceptions of the benefits of farming developed at all, for in the case of the Natufians and the Zwai Chemi hunter-gatherers subsistence seems to have been quite satisfactory. Anthropological studies of present-day hunter-gatherers, such as that by Richard Lee on the Kung bushmen of South Africa, show quite clearly that it is not a very harsh way of life and that only rarely is there great food shortage. Leisure time is apparently abundant and there are also fewer demanding daily commitments. Why should clearly successful hunter-gatherers settle down to village life and allow themselves to become tied to crops, to the risk of crop failure, to domestic animals and to the demands of their constant attention? This is a question that is at present not fully answered, but several hypotheses have been put forward which are summarised below.

If the hunter-gatherers and wild cereals and ruminants shared the same habitat a close living relationship of a symbiotic kind would have developed so that any 'experimental farming' would have further increased mutual dependence. The more settled people became the more plants and animals they would have had to tend and the less likely they would be to move with all their farming and food processing equipment. They would have come to live in permanent villages. (The nuclear zone hypothesis; Braidwood 1967.) The process of adopting farming might have been intensified by demographic factors. Once food storage was adopted there would be virtually no starvation. Primitive birth controls, such as infanticide, may have lessened and the better nutrition of the population may have prolonged and increased human fertility. Population expansion would have created pressures for more efficient food production, hence more crops would be sown and tended and animals more protectively herded. (The population pressure hypothesis; Boserup 1965.) If the optimal environments of the nuclear zone produced the greatest population expansion then emigration away would be inevitable if the people had lost their hunter-gatherer adapted population controls. If the population over-spilled into marginal areas, where traditional hunting and gathering were difficult, the people would be under pressure to find food. They might thus take with them the nuclear region plants and animals so that a food supply could be ensured. (The marginal zone hypothesis; Binford 1968.) These three hypotheses are not mutually exclusive. They may be taken together to explain why the cereals and ruminants of one small area of the Near East came to be the basis of the first farming and to spread out so rapidly from their centre of origin.

11.5   Neolithic farming communities

Between 8 000 and 5 000 BC farming practices became much more established in the Near East and began to displace the Mesolithic cultures. Investigations of contemporary sites during this period reveals not only the variety of types of settled community but also that hunting and gathering continued as well. The **Neolithic Revolution** in food production, as envisaged by Gordon Childe (1936) who coined the phrase, was not uniform nor indeed did it probably seem revolutionary at the time. But farming must have had some edge on the old way of life, even if it was just less trouble to live in one place all the time rather than to be continually on the move. Moreover, sedentism, the term used for a settled village life rather than a nomadic one, favoured the development of many cultural features besides farming. The clay models of animals and fertility symbol Venus figurines of this early Neolithic period foreshadow the further development of art and religion in the early civilisations.

At **Jarmo**, in Iraq, in the original nuclear zone there was, by 6 750 BC, a considerable village of 150–200 inhabitants. Goats and sheep were herded and barley and einkorn wheat were of the domesticated species form, whilst emmer was transitional from the wild cereal. Crude pottery containers and finely worked stone bowls have been found. Mortars and querns were in use for food processing and the presence of polished stone axes and adzes are indicative of a dependence on woodworking. Pigs, horses and wild cattle were hunted still and not domesticated.

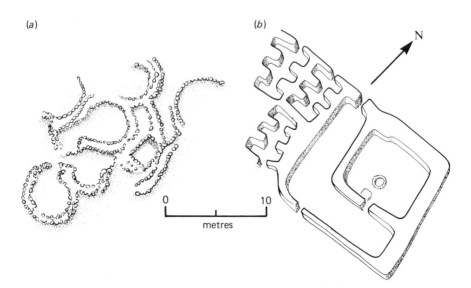

Figure 11.3   The evolution of rectangular buildings at Beidha
(a) level 6 of the settlement (7 500 BC) – circular plan stone huts with reed roofs, supported by posts, were clustered together with small rectangular storage areas between. Levels 5, 4 and 3, lying above, have progressively larger roomed houses with more rectilinear shape.
(b) level 2 of the settlement (6 000 BC) – the rectangular walled dwelling has a central hearth and outer corridor compound. There is evidence that the chambered corridors housed special craft and storage areas. (After Kirkbride, 1968.)

At **Abu Hureyra**, in Syria, a much larger settlement has been unearthed dating between 7 500 and 5 000 BC. Einkorn wheat, barley and lentils were grown and emmer wheat was later domesticated. There is evidence at this site on the edge of the Mesopotamian plain that irrigation was employed, harnessing a perennial stream to extend the cultivated area. Early in the settlement's history, gazelle, sheep and goats were herded but by 6 000 BC the gazelles declined and cattle and pigs enter domestication for the first time. The size of Abu Hureyra's community indicates some additional village involvement in trade. Obsidian, a volcanic glass that makes the finest microliths, was imported from Turkey along with agate and malachite stones for adornment and cosmetic use. Turquoise stones and cowrie shells indicate trade with Sinai and the Red Sea coast.

At **Catal Huyuk**, in Turkey, between 6 000 and 5 500 BC an even larger community had developed a town of mud-built pit dwellings, consisting of single rooms five metres square set around open courtyards. These buildings, unlike the earlier round dwellings, were roofed with beams and thatch and entered from above by a ladder. Catal Huyuk was again a trade centre, judging by the exotic artefacts discovered, but it is of greatest interest for being one of the first sites where hexaploid wheat is found. Again it is the earliest site at which cattle were undoubtedly domesticated, the remains of large numbers of young animals being found together with biface butchering tools on the town site itself. Although such large Neolithic settlements as this may have housed several hundred people most of the villages are not envisaged as having more than one or two hundred inhabitants at the most. For all settlements, agriculture, hunting and gathering employed almost all of the population. Trade was by reciprocal barter and the practice of crafts such as pottery and basketry was largely home-based. The large numbers of small shrines at Catal Huyuk, distinguished by burials and associated objects, indicates that religion was an important part of each household's life and not the province of a special priesthood. The equal size of all the dwellings can be taken to indicate an egalitarian society in which many resources were probably shared.

11.6 Domesticated animals

The ruminant herbivores (sheep, goats, cattle) are the most important domesticated animal group for they have the capacity to digest cellulose and thus do not compete directly for the same food resources as man. Ecologically, by their domestication, man has therefore directed more of the available food resources in his environment in his own direction than would have been possible by hunting alone. These ruminants have a natural sociability, or herd instinct, in the wild. This social feature is exploited in the leading and following that herding involves. The available archaeological evidence suggests that each ruminant herbivore species that was domesticated had one centre of origin and that their first domesticators relied upon just this one herd animal species for a long period before the subsequent variety of kept animals developed. Domestication would have involved selection for particular carcase features, skin and horn characteristics and that docility and tractability without which they would have been unmanageable. It would have been the awkward or aggressive beast that went first to be slaughtered. Whether the bones, unearthed by archaeologists, are thought to be of domesticated animals rather than hunted ones depends upon three factors. First, the age distribution of domesticated animal bones peaks at a stage of immature skeletal development, that is they are young animals culled from a more mature breeding herd. Secondly, their bones may differ in skeletal proportions from the wild species. Thirdly, domesticated ruminants have been shown to have an altered bone mineral crystal structure that can be seen microscopically.

Sheep, *Ovis aries,* were domesticated from about 9 000 BC from *Ovis ammon* the wild sheep of the Taurus-Zagros range. Today these wild animals prefer rolling hilly country and maintain a subclimax short grass pasture land. Domesticated sheep have largely lost their horns, or they are at least much reduced. They are shorter in stature and their mutton has a much higher muscle fat content. Wild sheep have long hair (kemp) and short underwool. Under domestication the wool has increased and the kemp decreased to give a warmer fleece. There is no evidence of wool weaving until 4 000 BC.

Goats, *Capra hircus,* are descended from the wild goats of south-west Asia. Found exclusively at some sites such as Ali Kosh, and later together with sheep and cattle at others, goats are believed to have been first domesticated in the Zagros mountains in about 8 000 BC. Although rocky mountain dwellers, under domestication they fulfilled an ecological role different from sheep, browsing from bushes and trees. Goats perhaps became more important as deforestation and the consequent environmental desiccation progressed in the Near East in the late Neolithic and early historic times for they can subsist on very arid marginal land. The balance of evidence points out the goat as the principal culprit in this 'desertification' process.

Figure 11.4   Wild goats showing the 'herd instinct' of leading and following, undoubtedly exploited by man in their domestication

Cattle, *Bos tauros*, were first domesticated from the wild cattle or auroch, *Bos primigenius*, of the Anatolian plateau, north of the Taurus Mountains in Central Turkey. Large, long horned and extremely fierce, they must have been most difficult to domesticate, but by late Egyptian times they had become, by artificial selection, short-horned and smaller in size. Probably first domesticated in 6 500 BC, they became the most important ruminant animal in lowland Mesopotamia and Egypt where the long grass alluvial plain pastures suited them better. Horn, thick hide, meat and milk were important products of cattle, but their unique contribution was to provide animal traction. Cattle-power released men from the land and extended the cultivable area of the early Mesopotamian civilisation.

Dogs, *Canis familiaris*, were undoubtedly domesticated by Mesolithic hunters from the small wild wolf, *Canis lupus*. This may have happened many times and in different places but the earliest Near Eastern remains date from 11 000 BC and hence is the very earliest animal domestication that occurred. Remains of dogs are very rare at early sites in the Neolithic and hence their presence cannot be assumed. The dog's role in hunting and subsequently herding is only surmise but might have been important in achieving the symbiosis between herd animals and man. The natural sociability of wolves enabled the early dog to respond to human society in their characteristically social way.

The pig, *Sus sus*, was domesticated from the wild boar, *Sus scrofa*. Being a non-ruminant omnivore its value as a domestic animal came late in the Neolithic agricultural revolution, being hunted but not domesticated until 6 500 BC. The omnivorous pig was useful as a scavenger on the village food surpluses, thereby returning waste to human consumption as useful meat and fat.

After the novel use of the ox, the adoption of other large mammals for transportation developed quite rapidly. The donkey was domesticated from the wild ass in early Egypt in 4000 BC but the horse and camel were not domesticated until the third millenium BC, in Central Asia and Southern Arabia respectively.

11.7 Domesticated plants

Cereal grasses are by far the most important domesticated plants because their mature fruits, or grains, are a concentrated form of edible carbohydrate and other valuable nutrients which can be stored. Wild cereal grasses are characterised by their smaller seed grain, firmly attached **glumes** and **bracts**, with hairy awns, and a central axis or **rachis** which shatters when the grain is ripe. These adaptations cause mature seed to fall, perhaps becoming attached to a mammal's fur for dispersal and then self-seeding into the soil by means of the attached hairy awn. Domesticated cereals have lost the shattering rachis adaptation, enabling the whole head to be harvested without loss of grain; the bearding of awns is often reduced; the glumes and bracts more easily detach and are winnowed off as chaff; there are more florets per head and grains are larger.

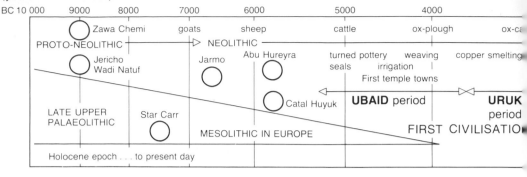

(years before Christ)

| BC 10 000 | 9000 | 8000 | 7000 | 6000 | 5000 | 4000 | |

Zawa Chemi   goats   sheep   cattle   ox-plough   ox-ca

PROTO-NEOLITHIC   ▷ NEOLITHIC

Jericho   Jarmo   Abu Hureyra   turned pottery   weaving   copper smelting
Wadi Natuf   seals   irrigation
First temple towns

Catal Huyuk   **UBAID** period   **URUK**
LATE UPPER   Star Carr   period
PALAEOLITHIC
MESOLITHIC IN EUROPE   FIRST CIVILISATIO

Holocene epoch . . . to present day

Archaeological identification of seeds clearly requires close reference to wild and domesticated species. The remains themselves are fragile. New techniques of excavated soil flotation have made possible the separation and collection of carbonised grains and floral parts, reduced to a delicate carbon replica by heating at the time of their preservation. Casts of cereal grains or plant impressions are found in clay and bricks, whilst in certain excavated tombs, such as those in Ancient Egypt, the grains themselves remain. Without the fine botanical technique implicit in these indentifications our knowledge would be minimal. Experimental genetics using wild species of grasses has demonstrated beyond doubt that the **tetraploid** emmer and **hexaploid** common wheat arose as **allopolyploids**.

Wheat. Einkorn, *Triticum monococcum*, was first fully domesticated in the mountainous regions of the Tauros–Zagros range. This is the distribution centre of its wild precursor *T. boeoticum*, *T. monococcum* being distinguished by its larger grain and non-shattering head. This latter feature, first recorded at Ali Kosh in 7 000 BC implies that by then the heads were harvested intact, threshed and winnowed and the seed grain later sown deliberately. Emmer, the natural tetraploid wheat, in its wild form *T. dicoccoides*, was gathered by the Natufians in Gallilee as early as 11 000 BC but does not appear in its domesticated form *T. dicoccum* until 7 000 BC at several sites outside its distributional centre in the Gallilee region. The hexaploid *T. aestivum*, common wheat, arose during cultivation as early as 5 500 BC as an allopolyploid of emmer and a wild grass; this is the flood plain irrigated wheat upon which Mesopotamian and Egyptian civilisation thrived.

Barley was domesticated early in the Levant or in the nuclear region between 7 000 and 6 000 BC; there is also a transition from two row to six row varieties thereby increasing yields. The species is tolerant of a wide range of climatic conditions and initially was quite as important as the wheats.

Legumes. Pulses were originally gathered but later enter cultivation in the Neolithic of the Near East. Peas were derived from a wild species that still grows as a weed of cereal crops. Lentils show a progressive increase in seed size during the Neolithic (2.5 to 6.5 mm diameter) and still grow wild today in natural stands, like the wild cereals, and may have been domesticated in a comparable way.

The Neolithic, by all pace of change that preceded it, was indeed a revolution. Ecologically man became more closely bound with his food source

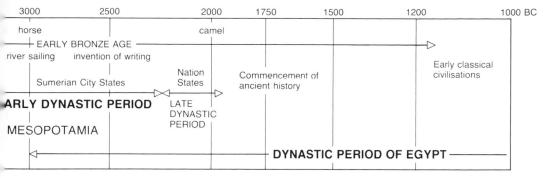

horse   camel

──┼─ EARLY BRONZE AGE ──▷

river sailing   invention of writing

Early classical
civilisations

Nation   Commencement of
States   ancient history

Sumerian City States

ARLY DYNASTIC PERIOD   LATE
                                DYNASTIC
                                PERIOD
MESOPOTAMIA

◁── **DYNASTIC PERIOD OF EGYPT** ────────

species in a way that modified the lives of both; the first domesticated sheep and cereals could no more have survived without man than man could subsist without them. Hunter-gatherer ways thus became harder to return to. Hunting, once a livelihood, now became a sport. Gathering diminished, as gardens with herbs and orchards with fruit grew up around the now-permanent home base, the Neolithic village.

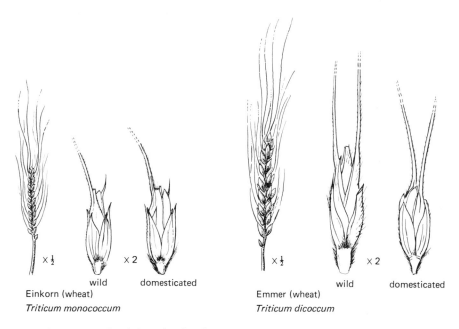

×½	×2		×½	×2
	wild	domesticated		wild	domesticated

Einkorn (wheat)   Emmer (wheat)
Triticum monococcum   *Triticum dicoccum*

Figure 11.5   Ear and spikelets of early wheat
In the early domestication of wheat from wild grasses the cultivated forms had denser, more compact heads, less tendency to shed seeds, shorter, less hairy awns and a heavier, shorter broad grain. (after Jane Renfrew, 1983.)

12 The origins of civilisation

Today we tend to use the term 'civilised', both in contrast to some notional primitiveness, and to describe the standards of living, of education, technology, and arts and of moral or social development which we find in our own society. This usage is derived from its original meaning which was to describe the characteristic attributes of the dwellers of cities, for the earliest cities made possible developments in human culture which have transformed society. Life in our modern cities may not seem 'civilised' yet we need to be reminded that urban living gave rise to **civilisation**, the most complex cultural evolutionary change in the whole of mankind's history.

Although early civilisations were based on city dwelling these could only have sprung from a rural technology and rural society capable of supporting them. It is a singularly important fact of human ecology that cities could not have arisen without the Neolithic revolution in which domesticated plant species provided a **food surplus** that could be stored. The availability of surpluses freed individuals from agricultural work for other trades and roles in their society. These new activities centred on single localities to which the surpluses of food were transported. Because these new societies evolved a **hierarchical social structure** different from those of primitive rural communities and because the potential energy of the stored food surplus was not equally distributed within the society, but according to hierarchical status, human societies entered for the first time into the complexities of economic and political realtionships. In **Mesopotamia** and then **Egypt**, the wheat and barley surpluses, from irrigated land, was transported to service these centres of population density, unequalled before in human prehistory. Neolithic farmers of the **Indus** adopted rice, as a wetland cereal substitute for wheat, which in its turn became the economic base of the oriental civilisations. In the New World, apparently quite independently, maize domestication gave rise to the **Central American** civilisations, and in the high **Andes** the potato did the same for the Incas. The beginnings of civilisation were thus marked by man's capacity to store large amounts of surplus food energy and by his ability to organise himself into larger denser communities within which the redistribution of goods and materials for each individual's livelihood could take place.

12.1   The development of hierarchical society

Compared to man's hunter-gatherer past, the most distinctive feature of civilised societies are their hierarchical rather than egalitarian nature. Within a small band there would be only slight differences of status, varying with an individual's age, sex, skill and personality. Within much larger societies there has been diversification and amplification of these differences. Although social evolution is complex an attempt is made here to give a simplified description of this increasing complexity of hierarchy and the inherent trend towards greater size, greater specialisation and more complex means of social integration that civilisation has produced. Elman Service (1962) recognises four stages of cultural organisation; **the band**, the **tribe**, the **chiefdom** and the **state**. The description of these stages provide an important theoretical background to archaeological discovery.

The band is a small territorial hunting and gathering group of 30–100 members. Sex, age and skills differentiate status more than anything else. There is no political or economic specialisation. Intermarriage between neighbouring bands is common. Sharing of all resources makes this society egalitarian. This is the type of society in which man has lived for longest, in which few remain today and which largely disappears on the adoption of agriculture.

The tribe is distinguished by the integration of local groups into a larger single society comprising from hundreds to a few thousands of individuals. Cutting across local groups are such social structures as clans which may govern marriage. Age groups commonly organize together, such as into groups of warriors or elders. Generally the economy is agricultural and egalitarian though there will be more differentiation of status, for example between wives in a polygamous marriage. Tribes may develop more strongly in response to the external threats of other tribes or different societies. Warfare rarely consists of more than skirmishes.

Chiefdoms are distinguished by greater hierarchical groupings in which rank is associated with both privileges and obligations. The hierarchy centres on the chief and an individual's position in the society is related to his or her descent or kinship and to status earned. There is more division of labour within society. There must therefore be distribution of food to non-food producing members, like craftsmen, and the chief's status ensures that this occurs. In return all members of society must contribute by their labour, but in redistribution of the products the chief has patronage and thereby particular groups or individuals may be given greater shares and hence have higher status. The population may be of many thousands of people who are drawn together by established economic, social and religious activities. Organised campaigns of warfare may occur.

States are distinguished by their greater complexity than chiefdoms and the concentration of economic and political power in ruling groups. There are at least three levels in the hierarchy, often more. The middle levels of the **bureaucracy** exercise political power on behalf of the rulers. There are defined **social classes** and often economic and social differences between the individuals in different trades and professions. Patronage by state rulers makes possible great investment in art and technology resulting in the development of increased communications and knowledge. Decisions by rulers are communicated through the bureaucracy. These decisions are often formalised into codes of law and are then supported by religious, cultural and personal attitudes. States are territorial and exercise a monopoly in the use of force to either restrain members of the society or to encourage them to participate in organised warfare against neighbours, for which the state also often maintains a professional fighting force.

12.2   Early Mesopotamian towns and cities

Against the background of social evolutionary classification outlined above, the archaeological evidence can be assessed. How did civilisation develop in Mesopotamia, in this very first instance? What environmental factors or forces in society produced the complexity?

Advanced farming villages (6th millenium BC)

Around 6000 BC villages of farming people began to spread down from the Zagros highlands into the hotter more arid Mesopotamian plain. Development of settlements would have been alongside the rivers into these drier areas, utilising increasingly the perennial streams for **irrigation** of agricultural land. Colonisation could not have been easy for in the alluvial plain the rivers often changed their course when in flood, but the environment was biologically productive if tamed. Known by their distinctive pottery, several **Samarran sites** from the 6th millenium have been investigated in this fringe region of the Mesopotamian plain. The excavated buildings are of sun-dried mud-brick with plastered floors and walls, no longer round in shape like those of the shifting villages but now rectangular. A rectangular shape more easily allows further built additions to a home. Here for the first time, of the many dwellings excavated, some individuals' homes had been much more extended and had been made with sizeably larger rooms. This has been interpreted as implying some social stratification in the village with a few higher status individuals. Much larger dwellings associated with religious artefacts and burials suggest the development of a specialised priesthood. The burial of infants together with richly ornate statuettes suggests the existence of a ruling family chiefdom, for such burial could not be afforded for every infant death. The organisation required for any irrigation management would have needed some central authority, control and cooperation, to be fully successful. Bureaucracy perhaps had its beginnings here. We know that property concepts were developing, for distinctive seals and seal impressions are found on the pottery in which the surplus food was stored.

Temple towns: the Ubaid and Uruk Periods (5500–3000 BC)

On the earliest town sites of the Mesopotamian plain it is clear that settlements were on no previous occupation site and that very substantial centres of population grew up beside the canalised water courses on the desert fringe. Embankment of these water courses to prevent changes of course was essential, for the eventual breakdown of irrigation systems is testified to by the isolation of many archaeological sites far from present-day water courses. Pottery remains show that the culture of the earliest settlers of this region slowly evolved over thousands of years to give rise to the later Sumerian civilisation in which writing was developed. In these earliest of Mesopotamian plain sites there was a small, slightly raised, temple building covering 25 m², but at higher and later levels of occupation the temples become larger and more raised on great temple mounds of mud-brick. In the ancient city of **Uruk**, perhaps the first true city anywhere in the world, the earliest temple area was 500 m² and the latest a massive 4800 m². These enormous buildings, made of

Figure 12.1   Remains of the ziggurat (temple mound), Uruk

sun dried mud-brick, were clearly the centre of political power as well as religion. Later Sumerian writings indicate that the most important religious ceremonies related to agricultural fertility. If we can presume that there were religious creeds governing social behaviour and fairness, a formalisation of the **group altruism** of the band, the temple was most probably the centre of the redistributive economy. The temple administrators most probably kept records and calendars and advised farmers on such things as planting dates. The growth of defensive structures is a marked feature of these first cities. Even as early as Natufian times, in 8 000 BC, the trading and cereal gathering people of the Levant fortified the very first settlement at Jericho to protect their traded goods. **Opportunism**, seizing the main chance, is a strong cultural adaptation of hunter-gatherer man. The existence of stored food and materials thus became tempting prey for a less favoured neighbour to pillage, particularly for herding nomads, who undoubtedly carried out occasional skirmish attacks.

The Sumerian City States: the Early Dynastic Period (3 000–2 300 BC)
So successful were the larger temple towns that some twelve of them evolved into even larger city states. The power of these cities extended well into the supporting countryside around. At the beginning of this period canals were dug, many kilometres from the Tigris and Euphrates rivers, for the extensive irrigation of land and for transport by reed boat. The organisation of this water control technology operated as a positive feed-back on the growth of the city state. At the centre of power in the redistribution of goods the temples were still clearly important, but at the start of the **Sumerian Dynasty** the archaeological record reveals a consistent growth of very large dwellings, which would appear, from their later evolved form, to be palaces for each city's king. Slowly

political power was transferred from the temple to the palace. Great artistic achievements took place and massive earthworks and monuments were constructed most probably now with much slave labour. The earliest historical records of the Sumerians describe organised warfare between cities, attested to by the massive city walls. Uruk now had nine kilometres of city wall enclosing 400 hectares with an estimated 100 000 inhabitants. The development of writing, on clay tablets, and the rich remains in the Royal Cemetery of the neighbouring city of **Ur** are an abiding testimony to the cultural peak of this period. But against these cultural achievements one is soberly reminded of the extensive slavery and ritual killing of servants of the King that is recorded for this time.

Sumerian and Akkadian Nation States: the Late Dynastic Period 2 300–2 000 BC

The city states by competition, by conquest and a commonwealth of enterprise slowly fused into the first nation states before the close of the 3rd millenium BC. Each city retained its ruler but an overall empire was maintained by military conquest and the payment of tribute. This information now comes to us from contemporary and subsequent written records thus marking the passage from prehistory to the historical era. The nomadic herdsmen of the western semi-deserts were the main predators upon the settled Sumerians, but many of these nomadic Akkadians were undoubtedly assimilated into city society. History relates how Sargon, an assimilated Akkadian, became the first ruler of this empire and ruled from the Persian Gulf to Turkey in 2 200 BC. At the collapse of the whole dynasty in 2 000 BC a Semite called Abraham departed from the city of Ur. It is a telling end to prehistory, and to the beginning of ancient history, that the founding father of Islamic and Judaic civilisation left Mesopotamia with his own received story of the origins of mankind, in the Garden of Eden, and with folk memories of those terrible Mesopotamian floods.

12.3   Technological evolution

Materials – The earliest civilisations of Mesopotamia and Egypt were essentially stone-age cultures, for although metal working came early in the Near East Neolithic effective metal tools were slow to replace stone ones. Raw copper was first cold beaten in Turkey as early as 6 500 BC. Smelting of the green ore had begun by 5 000 BC but alloying copper with tin to make the melting point lower and the alloy, bronze, hard did not come about until the temple towns developed after 5 000 BC. Early metal axes were imitations of their polished stone counterparts and probably less used initially, for their cutting edge was relatively soft. Unlike stone, however, they could be recast and once alloying and the techniques for metal work were perfected bronze became highly valued as a material for tools of all kinds. Bronze working may have accelerated in Mesopotamia for there was a great shortage of good stone for tools. What they lacked in stone the Sumerians compensated for by their ubiquitous mud and clay, in the form of sun-baked bricks and kiln-fired pots. Turned pottery was produced on a slow wheel disc as early as 5 000 BC. This Ubaid pottery is boldly painted and simple in design. During the later Uruk

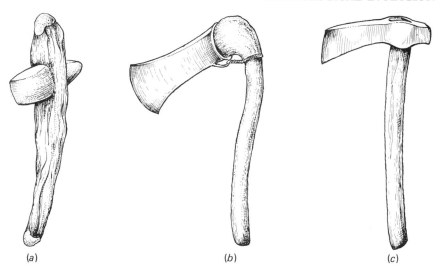

Figure 12.2   The technological evolution of the axe
(a) Neolithic ground stone axe head set in wooden handle
(b) Bronze Age socketed bronze axe on wooden shaft
(c) Iron Age Roman axe head attached to a wooden handle (after Le Gros Clark)

period, from 3 800 BC, a faster spinning wheel developed. Fired pottery equalled stone in its hardness, even to the extent of making hammers and nails, but had the great advantage over stone in its ease of design. Technology became more inventive and diversified. Wool and flax were both woven in the early Ubaid temple towns, flax perhaps being the first fibre to be used in loom weaving. Reeds were of undoubted importance in building, basketry and boat making.

Energy – Man's operative efficiency was increased not so much by new materials but by new developments in energy manipulation. Surpluses of wheat and barley were the fuel on which the human muscle power of the early towns and cities depended. From 3 000 BC dates were grown in huge palm groves which took many years to mature, and thus required careful planning, but their food energy yield was considerable, the fruits being also easily stored and transported.

Extrasomatic energy sources were also tapped. Cattle were the predominant domesticated ruminants of Mesopotamia being present from 5 000 BC. They were harnessed to simple wooden ploughs and sledges a thousand years later; the invention of the ox-cart followed at about 3 500 BC. The wheeled cart ingeniously reduces the frictional energy losses that early sledges and rollers suffered from. The **ard**, the earliest plough, consisted of a wooden hoe drawn through the ground by an ox. This extended the cultivable land which in turn increased the energy yields from farming. Ox-power may also have been used to move earth in canal building, in raising water for irrigation and in transporting food to the cities. All these uses of animal energy saved human energy on the land and enabled its diversion to the cultural developments of the city.

Figure 12.3   Babylonian mural
Male scribes are shown recording, on wet clay tablets, transported goods and livestock (800 BC).
Note the figure at the top herding both goats and sheep. Oxen are shown yoked to a simple cart
carrying a woman and children. Note also the date palm widely grown in Mesopotamia by this
period.

Water transport was important, requiring much less energy inputs than
transport by cart where frictional losses are considerable. Wind power was
exploited in sailing the rivers as early as 3 000 BC. Solar energy was utilised in
crop drying, for storage, and in mud-brick construction. Fire was utilised in
cooking, in pottery kilns and smelting.

Communications – Visual communication has always been important to
man. From our present studies of art amongst primitive peoples and of art in
the Upper Palaeolithic it is clear that the art of Mesopotamia and Egypt was a
grand continuation and flowering of a long tradition. These works of art
besides being bold, imaginative and mystical are also increasingly naturalistic.
This is peculiarly so in Egyptian and later Mesopotamian mural paintings of
everyday scenes, as well as in the fine engraving and statuery of human

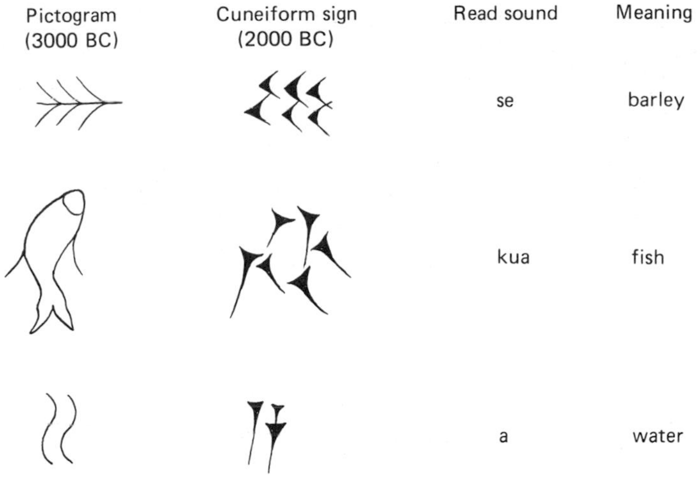

Pictogram (3000 BC)	Cuneiform sign (2000 BC)	Read sound	Meaning
		se	barley
		kua	fish
		a	water

Figure 12.4   An example of the cuneiform script

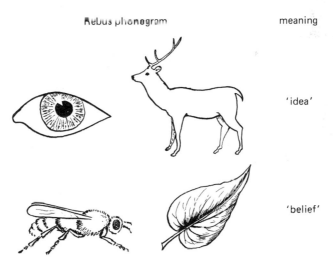

Rebus phonogram   meaning

'idea'

'belief'

Figure 12.5   How, in English, pictograms for familiar objects may be used as compound phonograms for expressing an abstract meaning

figures. However, it is the invention of writing, perhaps the triumph of the Sumerian dynasty, that brings prehistory to a close. From as early as the Upper Palaeolithic, marks made on bones have been interpreted as calendar records. In the early working of clay, seals were used to designate ownership or perhaps a maker's identity. By 3 000 BC picture signs, or **pictograms**, represented the important objects to be communicated as sketched on clay tablets. The latter could be dried and kept to form a permanent record. Two major innovations converted this recording system to one of writing. First, the 2000 pictograms depicting different objects were reduced to a more manageable number by combining pictures together to make words compounded from the basic

Figure 12.6   A cuneiform tablet (actual size)

pictogram sounds. Once a pictogram evolves into a 'sounding' word symbol it is called a **phonogram**, for it no longer conveys the meaning of the originally depicted object. This process is known as the **rebus principle** and is illustrated in Figure 12.5 for two English words, 'idea' and 'belief', which would be hard to express by one pictogram. The second parallel development was the substitution of the pictogram or phonogram by an abbreviated script. Thus the picture symbols of 3 000 BC became the **cuneiform script** of the Sumerian scribes a thousand years later. By sequencing the script symbols in a line words could be written, rather than drawn, and read as the language was syntactically spoken. Sumerian script contained about 600 characters some of which were read as representing objects and some as representing sounds to compound words. Each character was built up from wedge-shaped (cuneiform) marks impressed in the clay tablet. Writing made it far easier for separated communities to cohere together as one large society, with common laws and customs. By 2 350 BC the earliest written codes of law were established which curtailed the power of the wealthy, reduced the growth of bureaucracy and established the rights of citizens. Writing improved the keeping of records, calendars and accounts of formal events, as well as allowing the bureaucracy to levy taxes in a just and systematic manner. The invention of writing produced the beginnings of recorded history and the expansion of human knowledge.

Material and energy efficiency in the new technology enabled surplus food and products of craft industry to be exported from Mesopotamia. Communications were evidently widespread over much of this area of the world in 2 000 BC, and the raw materials for its technology were traded back. Bitumen, flint, limestone, basalt, tin and copper were imported for manufacture of goods, whilst gold, silver, gemstones and ivory were fashioned into the treasures of antiquity. Today, four thousand years later, our knowledge of the world, our continued exploitation of materials and energy and increased efficiency of communication and travel have only increased in amount and complexity from when history first began.

13 The biological characteristics of man: a conclusion

There is no more fundamental question for us personally than 'What is man?'. There is of course no one answer, but we can make concise statements of a descriptive kind on the biological characteristics of mankind today.

Classification

Modern Man, *Homo sapiens sapiens*, is polytypic, with many local forms and races, showing polymorphism of many genetic characters; but the one species, although so varied, has a single gene pool. The genus *Homo* is used to describe those species of distinctly human form and nature. The beginning of the genus is thus relatively indefinable in time, but man in this sense is at least $2\frac{1}{2}$ million years old. The species name, *Homo sapiens*, is used to define men with fully enlarged brains and sophisticated culture, making the species about half a million years old. All modern men are of the subspecies *Homo sapiens sapiens* typified by forms prevalent for the past 35 000 years. Man is the only surviving species in a once more diverse family of upright walkers, the hominids, and is now most closely related, in taxonomy, to the living African apes, for like man these also are hominoid, catarrhine, anthropoid primates.

Anatomy

Man is the only living upright bipedal hominid. The legs are relatively long, have an arched foot and an enlarged adducted big toe (hallux) which is not opposable to the other toes. The pelvis is broad with expanded ilia for gluteus muscle attachment. The femurs incline from the hip towards the midline at the knee. The sinuous spinal column is held vertically, not curved forward as in apes but having the characteristic retroflexions in the neck and lumbar regions. The shoulder and arm are highly mobile, the hand prehensile and finely opposable. The thorax is broad not deep. The erectly held head is almost balanced on the neck, necessitating only slight supporting neck musculature. The foramen magnum is beneath the skull. The cranial volume is approximately 1.4 litres, which when scaled for size is a brain volume to body weight ratio unequalled amongst primates. The cranial bones are rounded over the brain which has much enlarged frontal, temporal and parietal lobes and marked cortical folding. The face is drawn under the high forehead, there being no marked brow-ridges. The teeth are much reduced for a hominid, are even in the tooth row, and arranged in a parabolic arcade. The last molars are very late to appear. The reduced lower jaw is strengthened by a protruding chin. Body hair is especially thick on the head, but elsewhere hair shafts are thin and short to the extent of apparent nakedness. There is a marked sexual dimorphism of secondary sexual characters. Sweat glands are numerous.

Physiology

There is a prolonged pregnancy resulting in the birth of a large-brained yet still under-developed helpless infant. There is further delayed puberty hence longer childhood and a longer life span than any other primate. Brain physiology is highly complex, the production of learned syntactic language, and the degree of fine motor control of face and hands being special features. Learning and memory are prodigious and thought and 'self' consciousness, if not unique to man, are unique in their extent. The skin is a very specialised and efficient thermo-regulatory organ. Sexually, breeding may occur at any season and females have no oestrous period. Diet is not at all specific and feeding is omnivorous.

Behaviour

Infants are completely helpless at birth and depend upon a long period of learning and socialisation, which in fact continues through life. Gestural, facial and vocal signalling are complex, largely culturally developed and exclusively so in the case of the syntactic language in speech. Body adornment for utility, comfort, ritual or epigamic display is common (i.e. clothes, make-up, hairstyles.) Males and females are strongly pair-bonded for many years, family or kinship groups collecting into larger and larger social units. The largest societies are extremely complex and hierarchical. Social behaviour is both altruistic and sharing yet keenly opportunistic and competitive. Communal care and communal aggression are, by animal standards, extreme (from hospital to the H-bomb). The individual's thought, reflective self consciousness and inventive imagination find powerful social expression in the knowledge, moral order and cultural developments of their society. Because behavioural adaptation is very largely cultural man has the behavioural plasticity to adapt to environments created by himself.

Ecology

Man has entered into numerous exo-symbioses with plants and animals, which themselves have evolved to provide human habitat requirements. Much food energy is channelled through these organisms to man in his diet. Other non-biological energy sources are exploited, particularly fossil fuels. Living and non-living environmental materials are used and modified by technology to improve the human environment. Despite this many resources are over-exploited and the environment polluted by technological products. Some human habitats are entirely man-made (cities). Competing species, disease organisms and parasites are largely controlled. Innumerable species and their habitats are destroyed in man's expansion of his own preferred environment. The characteristically exponential human population growth curve shows signs of being checked, by density dependent overcrowding factors such as community-imposed limits, lack of food resources and mutual community destruction in mass warfare. Stable adaptation to environment is barely keeping pace with the rate of environmental modification.

THE BIOLOGICAL CHARACTERISTICS OF MAN: A CONCLUSION

The author is aware of the danger of treating man in this rather cursory manner; describing the classification, anatomy, physiology, behaviour and ecology of ourselves as if we were yet one more biological species to be described. But for too long man has seen himself as being outside the animal world, as a creation for whom the rules were somehow different. Darwin's evolutionary theory and much recent biological science has stripped us of that privilege, for we are in fact bound closely to our biological past and now perceive more clearly how unfree we may be. Yet our knowledge of the origins of mankind, of the long history of successful adaptive change and of the very length of the journey through time must become a new inspiration to us. Our perspective on human history has been far too short. We shall need to think much more about our past if we are to direct successfully our future cultural and even biological evolution.

Appendix I
Index of nomenclature, synonyms and localities of anthropoids

As enormous confusion may arise over nomenclature, especially in reference to other texts, an index of synonyms and localities is given (over). Where a name is listed unchanged there is an asterisk to signify that this is the name used in this textbook and is the nomenclature now generally accepted for the species concerned.

The use and meaning of latinised names

All species have a generic name and specific epithet in the binomial system of nomenclature. This is true both of living species (bio-species), for which full description of the species is possible today, as well as for fossil species (palaeo-species) which are arbitrarily divided on the basis of their fossil form and to some extent their date. Two or more species within the same genus should share many common characteristics but be sufficiently distinguished in form, behaviour, ecology or position in time, to be regarded as discrete populations. Ideally all members of one species should have a common gene pool and be potentially interbreeding. As we are unable to assess this for any fossil species, the ascription of separate species status is based upon differences in characteristics that may best be explained by a lack of such gene flow between populations; that is, they really do not appear to have been the same. Once taxonomic status is agreed, i.e. whether the form is a new genus or species, the question of naming arises.

In naming (nomenclature), classical Latin or latinised terms are used to describe generic or specific attributes of importance. Thus the words *Anthropus* and *Homo* mean 'man' in the generic sense, whilst *Pithecus* means 'ape'. These may be combined together, as in the 'ape-man' name *Pithecanthropus*. Such root term names may be qualified by some prefix, suffix, or specific name epithet. These qualifying additions denote such things as size, form, character, locality, age or habitat. Thus *Gigantopithecus* is a giant ape, *Pongo pygmaeus* a diminutive one. In nature, *Homo habilis* is conceived of as 'handy', *Homo erectus* as 'upright' in posture, and *Homo sapiens* as 'wise'. In locality, *Australopithecus* is a 'southern ape' and *Sinanthropus* a 'Chinese man'. Locality is often emphasised in such specific epithets as *africanus, afarensis, pekinensis*, etc. Such terms in combination may appear rather forbidding: for example early Java man was once described as *Meganthropus palaeojavanicus*. The names of mythical deities such as *Pan, Rama*, and *Siva*, appear in the list, whilst the legendary ancestral Zinj people of East Africa are honoured in the name *Zinjanthropus*. A presumed habitat is described in the 'tree-ape' name *Dryopithecus*.

The rule of priority dictates that when a specific form is first described scientifically the name it is given should hold for the future provided that it is not subsequently shown to be already described in an earlier genus or species. This is a cause of much apparent confusion and more often than not newly described species and genera of fossil hominids have been redesignated to prior taxonomic groupings. Views of affinity and of interpretation of earlier described forms also change and hence nomenclature changes are inevitable. The nomenclature used in this book, asterisked in the list, is that most accepted today.

Name	Synonym	Location
*Australopithecus afarensis		Ethiopia and E. Africa
*Australopithecus africanus		South and E. Africa
*Australopithecus boisei	(but may be combined with robustus)	E. Africa
Australopithecus erectus	Homo erectus	
Australopithecus habilis	Homo habilis	
*Australopithecus robustus		South (& East) Africa
*Dryopithecus		Africa and Eurasia
Eoanthropus dawsoni	Piltdown man	British Museum
*Gigantopithecus		Asia
*Gorilla gorilla	(gorilla)	East and Central Africa
*Homo erectus		Asia, Europe, Africa
*Homo habilis		Africa (Asia?)
Homo neanderthalensis	Homo sapiens neanderthalensis	
Homo rhodesiensis	Homo sapiens (Rhodesian Man)	Zambia
*Homo sapiens neanderthalensis	(Neanderthal Man)	N. Africa, Asia and Europe
*Homo sapiens sapiens	(Modern Man)	Global
Homo soloensis	Homo sapiens (Solo Man)	Java
*Hylobates	(Most gibbon species)	South East Asia
Javanthropus soloensis	Homo sapiens (Solo man)	Java
Kenyapithecus	Ramapithecus	E. Africa
*Limnopithecus	(gibbon-type fossil)	E. Africa
Meganthropus palaeo-javanicus	Homo erectus (early)	Java
Palaeanthropus	Homo erectus (Heidelberg man)	Germany
Pan gorilla	Gorilla gorilla	
Pan satyrus	Pan troglodytes	
*Pan troglodytes	(chimpanzee)	West, Central and E. Africa
Paranthropus crassidens	Australopithecus robustus	South Africa
Paranthropus robustus	Australopithecus robustus	South Africa
Pithecanthropus erectus	Homo erectus (Java man)	Java
Plesianthropus transvaalensis	Australopithecus africanus	South Africa
*Pliopithecus	(gibbon-type fossil)	East Africa
*Pongo pygmaeus	(modern orangutan)	South East Asia
Proconsul	Dryopithecus (African sub genus)	East Africa
*Ramapithecus		Africa, Asia and Europe
Sinanthropus pekinensis	Homo erectus (Pekin Man)	China
*Sivapithecus		Asia
Telanthropus capensis	Homo erectus (early) (Swartkrans Man)	South Africa
Zinjanthropus boisei	Australopithecus boisei	

Appendix 2
Size and scaling in human evolution

As is pointed out in Chapter 8, brain expansion is a major feature in the evolution of modern man. The figure below illustrates this trend by means of a large sample of known brain volumes. Although absolute brain size is important its actual organisation and degree of cortical folding is more significant in an assessment of brain development.

Mean and 95% population limits for cranial capacities of hominids

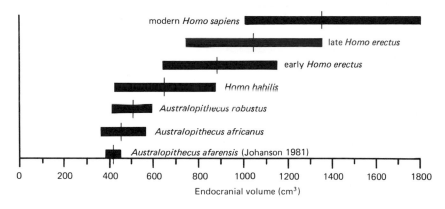

Endocranial volume (cm³)

(from Tobias, 1981)

As the larger an animal becomes the more brain tissue it needs for control of the body, one might argue that man is just more brainy because he is bigger! However, the figure below (from D. Pilbeam and S. Gould 1974) shows how brain volume and body size relate together for a range of size forms within each of three groups, the australopithecines, the *Homo* lineage and modern pongid apes, such as chimps and gorillas. On this scale the australopithecine man-

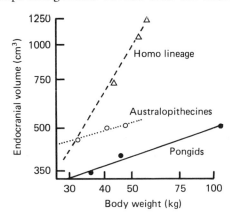

apes have clearly larger brains than true apes, but the human line hominids have quite markedly larger brains for their size increase.

The figure below shows a comparable scaling exercise for the australo-pithecines, *Homo* lineage and modern apes where the tooth area used in chewing and body size estimates are compared. The bigger the apes, or indeed the man-apes, become the proportionately larger were their teeth. The australopithecines are distinguished from the apes by their larger tooth area. However, in the human lineage, there is a negative correlation with the tooth area being absolutely smaller in modern man.

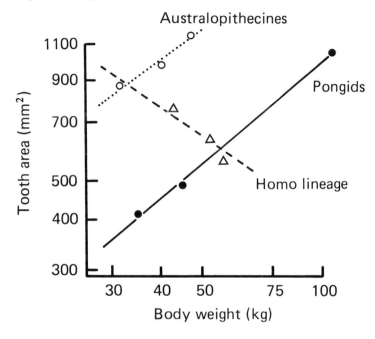

Further reading and references

* Good introductory texts to topics and recommended as further reading.
† Good sources of illustrations on evolutionary topics, human origins and prehistory.

New Scientist magazine is a good source of up-to-date information on new discoveries, though students should be cautious of its provocative journalistic style. *Scientific American* articles that have appeared as reprints and which are relevant to the subject of this book are listed below. These are obtainable from W. H. Freeman and Company Ltd, 20 Beaumont Street, Oxford.

†*Attenborough, D. (1979) *Life on earth*, Collins
 *Berry, N. J. (1982) *Neo-Darwinism*, Arnold
  Braidwood, R. J. (1975) *Prehistoric men* (8th edn), Glenview, Illinois
 †Brace, *et al.* (1979) *Atlas of human evolution*, Holt, Reinhart and Winston
 †British Museum (Natural History) (1983) *Our fossil relatives*, B.M.N.H.
  Burian, Z. and Wolf, J. (1978) *The dawn of man* (3rd edn), Thames and Hudson
†*Campbell, B. G. (1974) *Human evolution*, Aldine, Chicago and Heinemann
  Cole, S. (1970) *The neolithic revolution*, British Museum (Natural History)
  Darwin, C. M. (1859) *Origin of species*, John Murray (many editions e.g. Penguin 1968)
  Edwards, K. J. R. (1978) *Evolution in modern biology*, Arnold
  Eldredge and Tattersall (1982) *Myths of human evolution*, Columbia University
  Gould, S. J. and Eldredge N. (1977) 'Punctuated equilibria', *Palaeobiology* 3, 115
  Gould, S. J. (1978) *Ever since Darwin*, Andre Deutsch
  Gribbin, J. and Cherfas, J. (1982) *The monkey puzzle*, Triad/Granada
  Halstead, L. B. (1982) *Hunting the past*, Hamish Hamilton
  Hardy, A. (1960) 'Was man more aquatic in the past?' *New Scientist* 7, 642
 *Howard, J. (1982) *Darwin*, Oxford University Press
†*Johanson, D. C. et al. (1981) *Lucy: the beginning of humankind*, Granada
†*Leakey, R. and Lewin, R. (1977) *Origins*, MacDonald and Janes
†*Leakey, R. E. (1981) *The making of mankind*, Michael Joseph
  Le Gros Clark, W. E. (1971) *The antecedents of man*, Edinburgh University Press
 *Maynard Smith, J. (1976) *The theory of evolution*, Pelican
 †Moore, Ruth (1971) *Evolution*, Time Life Nature Library
  Morgan, E. (1972) *The descent of woman*, Souvenir Press, London
  Morris, D. (1967) *The naked ape*; Jonathan Cape
  Oakley, K. P. (1963) *Man the tool-maker*, British Museum
 †Oates, D. and J. (1976) *The rise of civilization*, Elsevier/Phaidon
 *Oxford Readers (32), Day, M. H. *Fossil history of man*,
     (41) Napier, J. *Primate locomotion*, (61) Napier, J. *Primates and their adaptations*
 *Pilbeam, D. (1972) *The ascent of man*, Collier-MacMillan

FURTHER READING

*Pfeiffer, J. E. (1981) *The emergence of man* (3rd edn), Harper and Row

Postgate, N. (1977) *The first empires*, Elsevier-Phaidon

†Prideaux, *et al.* (1973) *The emergence of man*, Time Life Books

†*Reader, J. (1981) *Missing links*, Collins

Redman, C. L. (1978) *The rise of civilization*, W. H. Freeman

Royal Society (1981) 'The Emergence of Man'; *Phil. Trans. Roy. Soc.* 292, 1–216

Scientific American Reprints:

    140, 549, 601, 602, 603, 604, 605, 606, 622, 630, 636, 643, 676, 682, 685, 686, 695, 700, 706, 709, 720, 722, 842, 844, 1070, 1246

Shaw, Thurstan (1981) 'Man's use of energy, *History today*, Jan. 1981

Shipman, P. (1981) *The life history of a fossil*, Harvard University Press

Simons, E. L. (1972) *Primate evolution*, Collier-MacMillan

Smith, Anthony (1974) *The human pedigree*, Allen and Unwin

†*Starr, C. G. (1973) *Early man: Prehistory and the ancient civilizations of the near east*, Oxford University Press

Stein, P. L. and Rowe B. M. (1974) *Physical anthropology*, McGraw Hill

*Stigler, R. *et al.* (1974) *The Old World: early man to the development of agriculture*, Thames and Hudson

Tanner, N. M. (1981) *On becoming human*, Cambridge University Press

†*Tattersall, I. (1969) *Man's ancestors*, John Murray

Van Lawick-Goodall, J. (1971) *In the shadow of man*, Collins

†Waechter, J. (1976) *Man before history*, Elsevier-Phaidon

Washburn and McCrum. (1978) *Human evolution, biosocial perspectives*, Cumings

*Weiss, M. L. and Mann, A. E. (1978) *Human biology and behaviour*, Little Brown

Wilson E. O. (1976) *Sociobiology*, Belknap/Harvard

Withers, G. R. A. (1971) *Charles Darwin and the theory of evolution*, Edward Arnold

Wood, B. (1976) *The evolution of early man*, Lowe

Young, J. Z. (1971) *Introduction to the study of man*, Oxford University Press

Young, J. Z. (1981) *The life of the vertebrates* (3rd edn), Clarendon Press

Index